the healing cookbook

Union Square & Co., LLC, is a subsidiary of Sterling Publishing Co., Inc.

Text © 2023 Gemma Ogston
Photography © 2023 Xavier Buendia
Illustrations © 2023 Carmen Ogston

First published in the United Kingdom in 2023 by Vermilion, an imprint of Ebury Publishing, part of the Penguin Random House group of companies.
This 2024 edition published by Union Square & Co.

ISBN 978-1-4549-5380-7
ISBN 978-1-4549-5381-4 (e-book)

For information about custom editions, special sales, and premium purchases, please contact specialsales@unionsquareandco.com.

Printed in China

2 4 6 8 10 9 7 5 3 1

unionsquareandco.com

Design: Louise Evans
Food stylist: Gemma Ogston
Prop stylist: Katie de Toney

the healing cookbook

Nourishing plant-based recipes to
help you feel better and stay well

Gemma Ogston

UNION
SQUARE
& CO.

NEW YORK

Contents

Feeling better starts here!   7

My healing essentials   10

Recipes for everyday healing   14

Recovery   23

Replenish   55

Staying Well   95

Supercharge   131

My Wellness Toolkit   167

Index   188
About Gem   191
Thank you   192

Feeling better starts here!

Now more than ever, so many of us are looking for ways to improve our health and boost our immunity, and the very best—and easiest—place to start is in the kitchen.

Paying attention to what and how we eat is such a simple way we can all take more control over our well-being. I truly believe that plants have the power to heal and I'm so excited to share this new collection of recipes and wellness ideas with you. My recipes are inexpensive and low effort, but packed with incredible ingredients that will make you feel instantly better. These are the recipes I cook and eat at home that keep me and my family feeling happy and healthy, and that help us get back on track when illness does inevitably strike. My food is always bright and colorful, using 100 percent plant-based whole foods along with some of my favorite magical superfood ingredients to boost your mood and supercharge your immunity.

I've studied plant-based nutrition extensively and am incredibly passionate about the amazing ways plants can be used as medicine to help heal us from the inside out. I know firsthand the incredible impact diet can have on how we feel, having been on my own journey to wellness when I began eating a plant-based diet ten years ago. Ever since making that life-changing decision, my energy levels have increased, my hormones have felt more in balance, my mood has lifted, and I get ill much less often. More recently, I've learned about the powerful effects specialist ingredients like medicinal mushrooms, plant powders, and seaweed can have, and I've seen some really impressive results.

For me and my family, eating plant-based whole foods keeps the focus on un-refined, healthy, and nutritious meals, with small amounts of animal products included—I still have eggs and a little dairy from time to time and my kids sometimes eat fish and meat, so I don't claim to be vegan. That is why my recipes occasionally contain honey or other non-vegan ingredients. To maximize the nutritional benefits of ingredients, it's generally fine to just wash or scrub fruit and veg without peeling them. The skin is rich in nutrients, so this increases your intake of vitamins, minerals, antioxidants, and fiber.

Whether you are currently experiencing a period of ill health, have specific recurring symptoms, or simply want to learn about ways you can support your immune system, I've included all my favorite ways to give yourself a head start, maximize your well-being, and take control over your health. It can feel like such an enormous and overwhelming topic, with a huge amount of information available out there, but I hope I've been able to bring together the key ideas to produce a practical guide to keeping well. Don't feel you have to suddenly overhaul your life! Even eating a few more veg-based meals, trying a couple of the self-care ideas, or adding a plant powder or two to your morning smoothie will bring you so many benefits—and you can build on it from there!

How the book works

The four main chapters—Recovery, Replenish, Staying Well, and Supercharge—are designed to support you through the four stages of getting back to peak wellness.

The first two chapters are for those times in our lives when we really need to take a step back and focus on our health—whether that's our physical or mental well-being. I strongly believe that we should all take more time to really tune in and listen to what our bodies and minds are trying to tell us they need—and then make sure we prioritize those needs. I know that when you're not feeling great cooking can sometimes feel like too much to tackle, so the simple, healing recipes in these chapters are super-easy to prepare while providing all the essential nutrients to assist your recovery and replenish your system once you are feeling a bit better. The recipes are full of active ingredients that will help ease some of the most common symptoms we experience during an illness, such as nausea, anxiety, sleeplessness, aches and pains, and coughs and colds.

When we're feeling better and more like our normal selves, we are often so relieved that this is often when we tend to neglect our diets or push ourselves more than we should. Actually, this is the ideal time to think about how we can help protect our wellness and keep our immunity in top shape. In Staying Well, I've included recipes that will keep you in optimum health and provide additional support to your immune system, building on the foundations of the previous chapters.

The fourth chapter is my favorite chapter in the book: Supercharge! The ideas here will take you to the next level in terms of future-proofing your immunity and wellness, elevating your mood, and supercharging your energy levels so you can live life to your full potential.

I've also included my list of Healing Essentials—the immunity-supporting pantry items I like to have on hand—as well as some basic recipes I make most weeks, such as my seeded bread and power-up hummus. And at the end of the book is an emergency Wellness Toolkit chapter. This is where I turn after a long day or week, when I need a quick helping hand. I've included revitalizing tonics, comforting easy recipes, and instant ways to get some extra nutrition.

As we all know, though, feeling in optimum health also includes how we feel mentally and emotionally. Often, when things start to feel out of balance, when we feel stressed or overloaded, or are experiencing low moods, these can quickly manifest into physical symptoms of illness, forcing us to slow down or stop. We need to start thinking of our wellness as a bigger picture. That's why, alongside the recipes, I've also included other key ideas to support your immunity and help you focus on your mental well-being. From simple self-care suggestions, breathing techniques, and how to achieve better rest, to the importance of good gut health, ways to find more balance in your life, how to identify your core priorities, and my tips for learning to enjoy an element of uncertainty in an ever-uncertain world, these are how I've learned to live in a way that is more aligned with my true self.

Dip into each chapter depending on how you're feeling, revisit sections whenever you need to, and know that wellness isn't always a linear pathway. It's inevitable you'll hit times in your life when you need to pay more attention to your health, but if you focus on setting some good foundations in nutrition, and include some much-needed downtime, plus a few bonus immunity boosters, you'll be putting yourself in the very best position to support yourself back to wellness, so that you can start feeling your best every day.

My healing essentials

I try to make sure my cupboards, fridge, and freezer always have a good supply of the immunity-supporting ingredients that I know will get my family and me back on track should we hit a period of ill health. The thing about not feeling your best is that illness almost always strikes when you're not expecting it, but you can still plan for it. Keeping a variety of these items stocked means I can create healing, nourishing meals and snacks to restore everyone to health and hopefully keep us healthy longer. I've also included some of my favorite non-food healing essentials to support all-around wellness and immunity.

Cans, jars, and packages
—
- **Grains:** bulgur wheat, quinoa, rice (white, brown, and Arborio), pearl barley, oats
- **Beans and legumes:** lentils, chickpeas, butter beans, kidney beans, black beans
- **Pasta and noodles:** pasta (regular and whole wheat), including some smaller shapes for adding to soups and stews
- **Noodles:** e.g., udon, whole wheat, and rice noodles
- **Dried fruits and berries:** e.g., goji berries, dates, raisins, cranberries, apricots, coconut flakes
- **Nuts and seeds:** e.g., chia seeds, sunflower seeds, hemp seeds, pumpkin seeds, flaxseeds, sesame seeds, almonds, Brazil nuts, macadamia nuts, peanuts, walnuts, hazelnuts, pecans, cashews

- **Plant-based milks:** unsweetened oat milk and almond milk (also see my recipe on page 14)
- **Coconut milk:** full-fat is creamier and more delicious
- **Canned tomatoes**
- **Canned fruit:** e.g., cherries, pineapple, clementines
- **Flour:** organic self-rising, all-purpose, spelt, and whole wheat (also gluten-free)
- **Nut butter:** palm-oil-free almond butter and peanut butter (also see my recipe on page 18)

Flavor boosters
—
- **Veggie stock/bouillon:** I make my own veggie stock from veg peelings and scraps and keep it stored in the freezer

- **Miso paste:** a great addition to soups and stews, it's amazing for gut health

- **Tamari or soy sauce:** I add this to stews, soups, and curries. It's quite salty so you may not need to add any extra salt.

- **Umami paste:** usually made from tomato puree, liquid aminos, dried mushrooms, and nutritional yeast, this will give any dish a real umami kick and a big nutritional boost. You can buy it from health food shops— or make your own. Add it to mayo, toss it in salad, or add a spoonful to stocks and stews.

- **Seaweed/sea moss:** a great way to get extra nutrients into stocks and stews and also give a salty taste to foods (see page 164 for more on seaweed and sea moss)

- **Nutritional yeast:** great to make vegan dishes taste cheesy and packed full of B vitamins, including B12 (also see my recipe for Vegan parmesan on page 19)

- **Maple syrup/honey/Demerara sugar:** the sweeteners I like to use

- **Cacao powder and good-quality dark chocolate:** essential in any kitchen! I use unsweetened cacao powder for making hot chocolates, smoothies, and cakes, and keep dark chocolate on hand to nibble on! Dark chocolate is rich in antioxidants and minerals that support the immune system and boost your mood.

- **Vanilla and almond extract**

- **Dried mushrooms:** these add a real depth of flavor and extra goodness to dishes (see page 109 for more on why I love mushrooms). I like to use dried porcini, shiitake, or oyster mushrooms. A little goes a long way, so you only need to add a few. If you're adding them to broths or stocks, you don't need to soak them. To use them instead of fresh mushrooms in pasta sauces or risottos, first soak them for 20 to 30 minutes in warm water, then drain.

- **Liquid aminos:** this has a similar taste to soy sauce or tamari but is less salty. It contains concentrated amino acids from soybeans. Amino acids are the building blocks of protein and are essential for so many functions in our body, including our immune system. Swap liquid aminos for tamari or soy sauce in any of the recipes.

Vinegars and oils
—

- **Vinegars:** apple cider (with the mother—so good for gut health), white, balsamic, red wine

- **Oils:** olive, coconut, sunflower, toasted sesame. I mainly use olive oil in cooking as it has a medium smoke point. It is also rich in antioxidants and is anti-inflammatory.

- **Garlic oil and chile oil:** to add flavor to salads, stews, or in cooking. Garlic and chile are natural immune-system boosters.

- **Herb oils:** put a few sprigs of rosemary or basil in a jar or bottle and fill with olive oil to infuse. They not only taste great, but many herbs are rich in antioxidants and have healing properties. Oregano and fennel oil are great for immunity support. I mainly use these herb-, garlic- and chile-infused oils to dress salads or to drizzle over pasta or bread.

Immunity-boosting superfoods
—

- **Medicinal mushroom powders:** to use in smoothies, energy balls, and teas (see page 109 for more on why I love mushrooms so much)

- **CBD oil:** to help with anxiety and aid more restful sleep

- **Herbal teas/sleepy tea:** I drink herbal teas throughout the day, so I keep a wide range on hand, including chamomile, nettle, fennel, mint, turmeric

- **Fruit and plant powders:** e.g., nettle, maca, and moringa to add to smoothies/juices for an extra nutrition boost (see page 170 for more info on these)

- **Vitamin D supplements:** taken daily, especially during the winter

- **Plant protein powders:** organic plant-based protein, such as hemp or pea, to add to smoothies, energy balls, sweet treats, or oatmeal or overnight oats. Stay away from whey protein, as it can cause digestive issues and tummy pains (whey is also a by-product of the dairy industry).

Herbs and spices
—

- **Immunity-boosting ground spices:** ginger, cinnamon, mixed spice, cardamom, nutmeg, turmeric, coriander, cumin

- **Bay leaves**

- **Chili powder**

- **Smoked paprika**

- **Garlic powder**

- **Mustard seeds**

- **Salts:** I like sea salt and flavored salts, such as garlic, herb, or smoked

- **Immunity-boosting herbs:** rosemary, thyme, sage, fennel, oregano, basil

Freezer
—

- **Frozen fruit and veg** are a great cheap option and mean you can enjoy ingredients when they're out of season. They're also so convenient and perfect for quick midweek meals. **Fruit:** avocados, berries, mango, bananas. **Veg:** peas, green beans, corn.

- Veggie stock and broths
- Leftover soups and stews
- Energy balls
- **Favorite plant-based ground meat and veggie sausages:** for quick family meals

My non-food wellness support kit
—

- **Echinacea:** I use a tincture that is wonderful added to teas or smoothies, especially when we have colds or feel like we are getting sick. It's an amazing herb that boosts the immune system, and is antiviral, anti-inflammatory, and high in antioxidants.

- **Essential oils:** I keep a selection and rotate according to what I feel I need, but my favorites are tea tree (antibacterial and boosts immunity), lavender (relaxing, reduces anxiety, antibacterial), eucalyptus (antibacterial and eases coughs), orange (uplifting; I use it in natural cleaning products), frankincense (for stress, anxiety, and inflammation, and to boost immunity).

- **Epsom salts:** for soothing achy muscles and for ultimate relaxation

- **Almond oil:** I use this as a base and add essential oils to it. It's great for using in the bath, on the body, and as a massage oil.

- **Candles:** I like to use naturally scented candles. I love lavender at night to help me feel relaxed

- **Body brush:** I use this daily before I shower to help with circulation, help get rid of toxins and stimulate the lymphatic system

- **Medicinal mushrooms:** e.g., chaga, tremella, lion's mane, reishi (see page 109 for more on medicinal mushrooms)

- **Vitamin supplements:** vitamin D, vitamin C, multivitamins for the kids

- **Mineral supplements:** zinc (supports the immune system), magnesium (helps with sleep)

- **CBD oil:** helps me sleep and manage stress. I use a few drops under my tongue when I need it or sometimes add it to a juice or smoothie. The oil contains cannabidiol, which comes from the cannabis plant, but it is not psychoactive and is totally legal. You can buy it from any good health food store or pharmacy.

- **Jade roller:** I am obsessed with my jade facial roller. It's perfect for a quick, cooling, calming facial massage to boost circulation, and it also helps with lymphatic drainage (see page 83 for my facial massage). It's even more refreshing and rejuvenating if you keep it in the fridge.

Recipes for everyday healing

These are my kitchen staples, the recipes I make at least once a week. Knowing I always have these in my cupboards and fridge means I have everything I need to put together a healthy snack, to form the basis for a quick supper, or to add an extra layer of nutrition to mealtimes.

Nut milks

—

You can buy some really good nut milks now (and they're great to stock up on for convenience), but you'll be surprised how extra-creamy and delicious—and easy—it is to make your own. High in healthy fats and selenium, you can use any nuts you like. Almonds make a great all-around milk, cashews are super-creamy, and Brazil nuts or hazelnuts will produce a very rich milk. You can use this method with seeds too, like pumpkin seeds or hemp hearts. I've also included my favorite superfood add-ons so you can supercharge your breakfast cereal or morning latte!

MAKES 4 CUPS | *Prep time: 5 minutes*
Soak time: 4 hours

1 cup nuts or seeds (cashews or almonds are best), soaked in a bowl of warm water, covered in a dish towel, for 4 hours or overnight (even 1 hour would be OK, especially if you are using seeds), then drained
4 cups filtered water
a pinch of salt

Optional flavor add-ins:
1 tbsp maple syrup
4 dates, pitted
1 tsp ground cinnamon
1 tsp vanilla extract

Superfood add-ins:
1 tsp ground turmeric + ½ tsp black pepper (all-around immunity booster and good for joint pain)
1 tbsp cacao powder (mood booster and rich in magnesium, calcium and zinc)
1 tbsp maca (hormone balancer and rich in iron)
1 tbsp nettle powder (rich in iron; boosts energy and improves sleep)

Combine the nuts, water, salt, and any add-ins in a blender. Blend on high for 3 minutes until creamy. Pour the mixture through a nut-milk bag, fine-mesh sieve, or double layer of cheesecloth set over a large bowl. Using the back of a spoon, press to release all the liquid. Pour the nut milk into a lidded bottle or jar and store in the fridge for up to 3 days. You can add the nut pulp to my granola recipe opposite or use it to make energy balls.

14

Goji granola

—

Goji berries give this simple breakfast snack added nutrition. They are packed with goodness and have been used for centuries in traditional medicine to protect against illness and are also very high in protein. I like to serve my granola with maca-infused nut milk (see opposite). Maca is an amazing superfood that helps balance hormones, so is great for PMS or perimenopausal symptoms.

SERVES 8 | *Prep time: 5 minutes*
Cook time: 20 minutes

2 tbsp unrefined coconut oil
⅓ cup maple syrup
2 tbsp honey
1 tsp vanilla extract
3 cups oats
⅓ cup seeds (I use pumpkin and sunflower)
⅓ cup sliced almonds
⅓ cup goji berries
¾ cup toasted coconut flakes

Preheat the oven to 400°F on the convection setting. In a large pan over low heat, melt the oil, maple syrup, and honey. Turn off the heat and mix in the vanilla, oats, seeds, and almonds. Spread the granola evenly over 2 baking sheets. Bake for 20 minutes, stirring halfway through, until golden. Mix in the gojis and coconut, and let cool. Store in an airtight container for up to a month.

Easy hummus + power-up extras

—

I don't need to tell you just how versatile hummus is. As a snack with chopped veg or crackers; on toast—maybe with sliced avocado, tomato, or scattered with some extra seeds; with salads, falafel, roasted veg; on the side of almost any meal . . . Hummus is one of those staples I honestly don't think I could live without. This is my basic recipe, and I've included some of my go-to extras for added nutrition and flavor.

SERVES 4 | *Prep time: 5 minutes*

14-ounce can chickpeas, drained and rinsed
2 garlic cloves
3 tbsp tahini
3½ tbsp water
3½ tbsp olive oil
juice of 1 lemon
a pinch of salt
½ tsp smoked paprika

Optional add-ins:
1 tbsp white miso paste (gut-loving)
1 tbsp peanut butter (extra protein)
1 tbsp seaweed flakes (extra nutrients)
½ roasted sweet potato, or 3½ ounces roasted squash (vitamin boost)

Add the chickpeas and garlic to a blender and blend for 30 seconds, then add the rest of the ingredients and blend on high until smooth. Cover and store in the fridge for up to 3 days.

Seeded bread

—

Perfect for sandwiches, toast (see my toast topper recipes on page 28), and to serve with any of the soups in this book, this bread is so delicious and full of goodness from all the seeds. I often also add 2 tablespoons of seaweed flakes (I use dulse) to the dry ingredients to make a delicious seaweed bread with extra nutrients (see page 164 for more on seaweed).

MAKES 1 LOAF | *Prep time: 10 minutes*
Cook time: 45 minutes

Dry ingredients:
2 cups whole wheat flour
½ cup toasted sunflower seeds
½ cup toasted pumpkin seeds
2 tbsp toasted sesame seeds
2 tbsp black sesame seeds
1 tsp baking powder
½ tsp baking soda
½ tsp salt

Wet ingredients:
1 cup water plus 1 tbsp lemon juice
¼ cup oil
⅓ cup honey

Topping:
¼ cup mixed seeds (sesame, pumpkin, sunflower)

Preheat the oven to 350°F on the convection setting. Grease and line a 9 × 5-inch loaf pan. Mix the dry ingredients together in a bowl. In another bowl, whisk all the wet ingredients together well, then pour into the dry ingredients. Mix until everything is well combined. Pour the mixture into the loaf pan and spread evenly. Sprinkle the topping seeds on top. Bake on the middle rack of the oven for 45 minutes. If you insert a skewer into the center of the loaf, it should come out clean. Let cool.

Cherry chia jam

—

Any ripe and juicy fruits are great for making chia jam, but I find berries and ripe stone fruits produce the best results. Cherries are one of the only foods that contain natural melatonin, so this healthy jam alternative will help aid natural sleep.

MAKES ⅔ CUP | *Prep time: 5 minutes*
Cook time: 5 minutes

3½ ounces frozen cherries
2 tbsp chia seeds
2 tbsp maple syrup

Place the cherries in a pan and cook over medium heat for a few minutes until they soften, then mash them. Add the chia seeds and maple syrup. Stir well. Pour the jam into glass jars. Allow to cool before placing in the fridge. It will keep for up to 4 days.

Nut butter
—

Nothing beats nut butter on toast, especially if you've been lacking in energy. It always reminds me of my childhood—with chopped banana on top! I usually make almond butter, as it has more vitamins and minerals than classic peanut butter, but you can use any nuts you like. Other nuts that work well are cashews, macadamias, and hazelnuts.

MAKES ¾ CUP | *Prep time: 15 minutes*
Cook time: 10 minutes

3½ cups raw almonds
¼ tsp salt

Extras:
(I like to add cinnamon, vanilla, and
   maple syrup)
¼ tsp ground cinnamon
½ tsp vanilla extract
2 tbsp maple syrup or honey
1 tbsp cacao powder

Lay the almonds on a baking sheet and roast for 10 minutes at 350°F (convection setting). Let cool. Transfer to a blender and blend until creamy, occasionally scraping down the sides as necessary. This may take up to 10 minutes but be patient and wait for the nut butter to get creamy. Add your extras and the salt, blend to combine, and then let the almond butter cool to room temperature. Transfer to a glass jar with a lid. Keep in the fridge for up to 2 weeks.

Variation: Homemade chocolate-nut spread Following the same method, use 2¼ cups hazelnuts, 2 tbsp cacao powder, 1 tsp vanilla extract, a pinch of salt, 2 tbsp maple syrup, and 2 tbsp melted coconut oil.

Immunity-boosting green goddess dressing
—

I could eat this by the spoonful. It goes with *everything*. Dress salads or warm roasted veggies, add to nourish bowls (page 121), or use it to top a simple baked potato. It's full of gut-healthy and immunity-supporting ingredients, like apple cider vinegar, garlic, honey, and herbs, with avocado to make it extra creamy and provide healthy fats.

MAKES 1½ CUPS | *Prep time: 5 minutes*

3 garlic cloves
1 medium avocado, peeled
¾ cup extra-virgin olive oil
7 tbsp water
5 tbsp apple cider vinegar
a handful of basil leaves
a handful of parsley, chopped
10 chives, chopped
2 scallions, sliced
juice of 1 lemon
1 tbsp honey
1 tsp salt

Blend all the ingredients until smooth and creamy. Keep in a lidded jar in the fridge for up to 2 weeks.

Gem's immunity-protection dressing

—

This is my absolute go-to dressing for salads and warm grain and veg dishes, like my Crunchy root tray bake on page 107. With apple cider vinegar, honey, garlic, ginger, and turmeric, it's packed with immunity-protection properties.

MAKES 1½ CUPS | *Prep time: 5 minutes*

¾ cup olive oil
½ cup apple cider vinegar
¼ cup water
3 tbsp light-colored honey
3 garlic cloves, chopped
2 inches fresh ginger, peeled and chopped
¼ tsp ground turmeric

Whisk all the ingredients in a bowl. Add to a jar with lid and shake. Or blend on high speed in a blender.

Vegan parmesan

—

You won't believe how delicious this is—even more delicious than the real thing! Plus, cashews are a great source of healthy fats and fiber.

SERVES 10 | *Prep time: 5 minutes*

2 cups raw cashews
3 tbsp nutritional yeast
1 tsp salt
½ tsp garlic powder (optional)

Add all ingredients to a blender and pulse until a fine meal is achieved. Store in the fridge for up to 2 weeks.

Toasted nuts or seeds

—

I always have a jar of these in the cupboard to add instant extra crunch, flavor, and nutrition to so many dishes—scatter them on salads, soups, or nourish bowls. They're a perfect quick snack too.

SERVES 8 | *Prep time: 5 minutes*
Cook time: 5 minutes

scant ½ cup brown sugar
1 tbsp toasted sesame oil
2 tbsp brown miso paste
salt and pepper (optional)
14 ounces mixed seeds (e.g., pumpkin, sunflower) and/or nuts (e.g., cashews, walnuts, almonds)
3 tbsp sesame seeds

Put the sugar in a small pan with ¼ cup water. Warm over low heat, until all the sugar has melted, then turn up the heat slightly until it bubbles. Remove from the heat immediately. Add the sesame oil and miso paste and stir well. Add salt and pepper if you like. Pour all the seeds and/or nuts into a bowl, then pour the miso caramel on top. Mix well until coated. Spread out on a parchment-lined baking sheet and let cool; they will get crispy. Keep in an airtight container for up to 4 weeks.

DRINK UP

Our bodies are around two-thirds water, so it's essential to keep properly hydrated in order to function at our best—but it's even more important when we're unwell. It's one of the simplest and most powerful ways we can support our immune systems to recover. Good hydration can help improve your energy levels and keep your digestion working efficiently; it can boost your focus and attention levels, flush out toxins and infections, keep your muscles and joints healthy, and assist in regulating body temperature—among many other complex functions in the body. Signs that you're not properly hydrated include headaches, dizziness, nausea, tiredness, dry lips and mouth, cramps, and dark-colored urine.

Most adults need around 6 to 8 cups of liquids every day, although this will change depending how hot it is and how active you are. Tap water (I prefer the taste of filtered) is obviously the easiest way to keep yourself hydrated, but it's not always the most appealing. Especially if you're not feeling great, or if you have symptoms of nausea, the thought of chugging several glasses of water can often make you feel worse. So get a little bit creative with your hydration and think about all the ways you can sneak in extra liquids. Here are some of my favorites.

1. A classic easy update to your regular water: fill a pitcher or bottle with water and add sliced citrus fruits for a refreshing zing, or chunks of chopped pineapple or mango for a tropical taste. Let it infuse for an hour or so, either chilled or at room temperature.

2. If your digestion feels a bit sensitive, or for something a little more savory, infuse your water with fresh herbs such as mint, rosemary, basil, or lemongrass. Herbs also contain medicinal properties. For a more intense flavor, infuse your herbs in boiled water to make a tea and drink hot, let cool, or serve iced. You can also use a combination of herbs and fruits (but only use hot water with lemon, as other fruit will go mushy). I also like to add seasonings such as ginger,

cinnamon sticks, and cloves—
these go well with orange slices.

3. Drink warm water mixed with
a spoonful of miso paste or
seaweed flakes, or a teaspoon of
sea moss for an umami flavor.

4. I love to add aromatherapy
oils to my water too—although
always check they're safe to
drink. Lemon, lime, wild orange,
rosemary, and fennel are just
a few of the oils you can take
orally and they have some great
medicinal properties.

5. Teas, juices, smoothies, soups,
and broths all add to your daily
liquid intake. For inspiration, see
my recipes on pages 33–34, 41,
62–63, 64, 113, 124, and 180.

6. Mother Nature gives you a helping
hand with your hydration in the
summer, with juicy tomatoes,
cucumber, watermelon, salad
leaves, and ripe fruits. Chop
them and keep some in the fridge
to snack on. Try the citrus salad
on page 30 for an extra dose of
vitamin C or dip cucumber chunks
in the hummus on page 15.

7. Ice pops are a great way to
rehydrate in hot weather. Freeze
diluted fruit juice in molds, make
a honey and lemon mixture, or
try freezing one of the juice

recipes on pages 33–34 or the
tonics on pages 172–4. Grapes
are also great to freeze and snack
on when you are dehydrated or
not feeling well.

8. If you've been sweating out a
fever or have had a stomach
bug, coconut water is a great
alternative to plain water as it
can help replace any essential
electrolytes you may have lost.
These help your cells function
properly and if they're out of
balance you can experience
muscle cramps. Sip on its own or
try my Rehydration juice below.

Rehydration juice
—

To replace essential salt, sugars,
and electrolytes.

SERVES 1 | *Prep time: 2 minutes*

⅔ cup fresh orange juice
juice of 1 lemon
juice of 1 grapefruit
1 cup coconut water
2 tbsp honey
½ tsp salt

Blend or mix all the ingredients
and drink right away.

CHAPTER 1

Recovery

Toast toppers 28
 Ginger + honey drizzle •
 Whipped miso butter •
 Marmite + mushroom +
 avocado toast

Vitamin C fruit salad 30

Easy juices 33
 Super-green nourish
 juice • Beet that flu juice •
 Sunshine carrot, orange +
 turmeric • Ginger, apple +
 lemon

Simple healing broth +
ramen noodles 40

Flu-buster golden
turmeric soup + brown
rice 42

Healing hydration 44
 Spiced saffron tea •
 Honey + ginger steamer •
 Medicine-ball tea •
 Three-minute ginger-aid

Tummy-loving simple
stew 49

Calming green soup 50

Steamed kitchari 52

Recovery

Too often, we don't give ourselves the proper time we need to rest and recover when we're ill. There's an unhelpful trend to always be on the go, always chasing the next hustle—although, thankfully, people are now starting to realize that never taking time out to relax and recuperate can cause all sorts of health issues, both physical and mental. I love to be busy and anyone who knows me will know it takes a lot to get me to sit still! But I've also learned that when I'm not feeling well or feeling exhausted or under the weather, it's absolutely essential to take a proper break and focus on doing everything I can to get myself back on track. If you ignore the signs, it can often take longer to recover and leave you feeling even more depleted.

So, this first chapter in the book is all about slowing down and STOPPING so you can focus on your recovery. It's about getting back to the basics of rest and good nutrition. It's about pressing that pause button just for a little while, so you can check in with yourself and really listen to what your body and mind need. These recipes are simple and no-hassle, nourishing, and comforting, but also easy to prepare and gentle on your digestion. There are simple self-care practices, such as morning mantras and calming breathwork, that I do every day—whether I'm sick or not—to help me find balance and keep me grounded.

Symptoms of needing to take a break can vary from person to person throughout their life. You could be experiencing a full-on illness that leaves you laid up in bed, be in physical pain from a chronic condition, or recovering from an injury, operation, or treatment. You could have a cold or flu, menstrual cramps, or digestive issues. Or perhaps you're experiencing a period of anxiety or low mood and need to take some time away from your daily life. Of course, always seek advice from your doctor and get the appropriate medical care and attention. But I hope this chapter provides you with some support when you need it in your journey back to wellness.

Stop

Imagine I am holding up a very large, neon STOP sign! That is your literal sign telling you it's time to take a break.

If you've turned to this section of the book, something inside you is letting you know that all is not well. Whether that's physically or mentally, listen to yourself and take the time you need to pause in your regular life so that you can focus on your recovery. Don't be one of those people who carry on regardless, crashing through and hoping you'll get better. That's a recipe for disaster.

You don't need anyone's permission to stop. It's an essential part of the ebb and flow of our life that at certain points you'll need to take a step back and slow down, to tend to your wellness and allow yourself to heal.

Your first step is to simply sit down, close your eyes, and take a deep, controlled breath. Turn your focus inside and really listen to what your body is asking for: are you tired? Have you been burning the candle at both ends for too long? Have you been ignoring a physical issue that now has stopped you in your tracks? Are you struggling emotionally and need to find some balance? Really listen to what your body and mind are telling you, and create the space to give them what they need.

Taking a break can, oddly, feel a bit overwhelming; but it's absolutely OK and in fact *essential* to take the time you need. Here are some ways to calm your mind and aid your recovery when you take a step back from daily life.

Don't be afraid to ask for help—and be specific. Most people are only too willing to lend a hand if they can, but they often don't know how to help, so give them a task. Think about what would help ease the pressure or anxiety. Maybe it's ad hoc childcare, picking up some groceries, changing the sheets on your bed, or cleaning the kitchen.

Screen limits. Especially if you're suffering with nausea, sickness, or headaches, cut right back on the scrolling, as flickering screens can make you feel worse. It can also make you feel more anxious if you're constantly checking in with what other people are doing.

Set a proper out of office. Even if you're self-employed, let people know that you're not going to be available for a little while. If you really can't leave things too long and it's making you more anxious worrying about it, let yourself check your emails and messages at one specific time each day and only get back to the really urgent things. Everything else can wait, and people will understand.

Work out your triggers. Strong smells, particular foods, or certain sitting or lying positions can all aggravate symptoms. Identify the things that make you feel worse and eliminate them as much as you can. Ask those around you to do the same.

Toast toppers

When you don't have the energy or appetite to cook and eat a proper meal, toast is the perfect solution. I always reach for toast when I feel too exhausted to prepare anything more complicated. Savory or sweet, the topping ideas are endless for simple ways to add some much-needed extra nutrition. As well as the below, try homemade Nut butter (page 18) with sliced banana for a boost of energy and to help increase serotonin levels, or my Cherry chia jam (page 17) to help you sleep. Whole-grain or rye breads contain extra fiber and nutrients—try my Seeded bread on page 17—but if your digestion is feeling a bit shaky, then simple white bread or sourdough is the gentlest to process. There's really not a lot that's more comforting than a warm slice of freshly made toast when you need some TLC.

Ginger + honey drizzle
—

When I was pregnant, I suffered terribly with morning sickness and lived off ginger (in anything). It really does help settle your stomach, so this topper is great for nausea, and the honey will give you a much-needed energy lift. Honey and ginger are also a great remedy for fighting colds.

Prep time: 2 minutes

Mix 2 tablespoons honey with 1 inch peeled and grated fresh ginger or ½ teaspoon ground ginger. Spread vegan butter over your toast, then pour the honey and ginger drizzle on top.

Whipped miso butter
—

Made from fermented soybeans, miso is packed full of probiotics so it's great if you have been experiencing any digestive issues.

Prep time: 5 minutes

In a food processor, combine a 4½-ounce block of vegan butter with 1 tablespoon white miso paste and process, or mash together in a small bowl, until smooth and combined. Spread a thick layer on hot toast and eat right away. The miso butter will keep for up to 2 weeks in the fridge.

Marmite + mushroom + avocado toast

—

This may sound slightly weird, but I promise it's packed with irresistible umami deliciousness—if you're a Marmite lover, you have to try it! Marmite is rich in vitamin B12 and if you're low in this it can make you feel weak and tired – a daily serving of Marmite will provide all your B12 needs. Avocados are very nutrient-dense, so if you haven't been eating much, then they are a great food to help regulate your appetite, while mushrooms are high in antioxidants and are a great all-around immunity booster (see pages 109–11 for more on mushrooms).

Prep time: 5 minutes | Cook time: 5 minutes

Heat 1 teaspoon olive oil in a skillet over medium-high heat, then cook a handful of button mushrooms, washed and sliced, until browned on both sides. Add a pinch of salt. While the mushrooms are cooking, toast 2 slices of your favorite bread. Mash 1 ripe avocado. Spread a thin layer of butter and Marmite on the toast, then add a layer of mashed avocado, then top with the cooked mushrooms.

Vitamin C fruit salad

Everyone knows how amazing vitamin C is for fighting off colds and flu, and this fruit salad is absolutely bursting with it. Ginger in the dressing will help settle any digestive issues, and turmeric has so many health benefits, from anti-inflammatory properties to all-around immunity protection. Make a batch of the salad and keep it in the fridge to snack on over a few days—the bright colors will give you just the pick-me-up you need if you're not feeling your best.

Dressing:
a pinch of salt
⅓ cup orange juice
zest and juice of
  2 limes
¼ tsp ground turmeric
a pinch of black
  pepper
½-inch piece fresh
  ginger, peeled and
  grated

Make the dressing by adding all the ingredients to a small bowl and mixing well. Put to one side.

Add all the fruit to a bowl and mix well. Top with the dressing and serve with optional toppings, if you like.

Salad:
2 pink grapefruit,
  peeled and sliced
3 large oranges,
  peeled and sliced
  (if you can get blood
  oranges, add one)
1 mango, peeled and
  cut into small wedges
2 kiwis, peeled and cut
  into 1-inch pieces

Optional toppings:
coconut yogurt
crushed nuts or seeds
  (also see Toasted
  nuts or seeds recipe
  on page 19)
grated orange zest

EASY JUICES

When you're feeling physically or mentally drained, I know how hard it can sometimes be to tick off your five a day. That's when I turn to juices for a supercharged dose of intense nutrition. Juices don't contain all the fiber you'll find in the whole ingredient or that you get in smoothies (see pages 62–63), but they are much more concentrated in terms of vitamins and nutrients, so they are great if you're not able to eat much, or as an addition to your regular meals.

You don't need a fancy juicer to make these—I just blend all the ingredients on high in a regular blender for 4 minutes, then strain through a sieve into a pitcher. Press down on the pulp to make sure you've extracted all the juice, then pour into a glass. Chill in the fridge for 15 minutes and enjoy. If your tummy is feeling a little sensitive, try to eat something small— like a piece of toast—before you drink one of these, as they could be a little acidic.

THESE WILL ALL MAKE TWO
1¼-CUP SERVINGS OF JUICE

Super-green nourish juice
—
This is my all-time-favorite healing juice. It's packed with iron from the kale, which is great for fighting fatigue. Kale is also rich in vitamin C—perfect if you have cold or flu symptoms. Ginger will help soothe nausea or sickness, and celery can help reduce inflammation if you're suffering from aches and pains.

Prep time: 15 minutes

1 bunch kale, leaves stemmed
   and chopped
2 celery stalks, chopped
½ cucumber, chopped
2 green apples, cored and chopped
1-inch piece fresh ginger, peeled
   and chopped
2 cups water

Beet that flu juice
—

The incredible vibrant color of this juice will immediately lift your mood. Beets are thought to work like an antihistamine, so they can help reduce allergy symptoms and ease congestion and sore throats. Carrots are anti-inflammatory and rich in beta-carotene, and citrus fruits are high in vitamin C—a classic immunity booster that may help bring down a fever.

Prep time: 10 minutes

3 beets, washed, peeled,
  and cut into chunks
2 carrots, cut into chunks
3 oranges, peeled and sliced
2 apples, cored and sliced
2-inch piece fresh ginger, peeled
a pinch of salt
2 cups water
juice of 1 lime, to serve

Sunshine carrot, orange + turmeric
—

This juice really is sunshine in a glass. I use coconut water, which not only makes it taste extra delicious but is also a natural source of electrolytes—including potassium, sodium, and magnesium—which are essential if you become dehydrated due to a fever or upset stomach. It can also help ease a headache. Turmeric is thought

to reduce all kinds of inflammation, including general inflammation caused by colds and flu.

Prep time: 5 minutes

3 medium carrots, cut into chunks
3 large oranges, peeled, seeded,
  and chopped
2 cups coconut water
1-inch piece fresh ginger, peeled and
  grated
½ tsp ground turmeric
a pinch of black pepper

Ginger, apple + lemon
—

A perfect juice if you're suffering from nausea and sickness. Ginger will help relieve your symptoms, and the mint and lemon will help settle your tummy. Coconut water will replace electrolytes lost through sickness. Sip slowly so you don't overload your stomach.

Prep time: 5 minutes

2 green apples, cored
1 lemon, peeled and seeded
1-inch piece fresh ginger, peeled
1 handful fresh mint leaves
2 cups coconut water

CHECK IN WITH YOURSELF

While you're in recovery mode, keep checking in with yourself to assess how you're doing. Often when we're not feeling well especially if we're stuck in bed, our minds can start to race, and it's easy to get into an unhelpful spiral of negative thinking or anxiety that can make us feel worse. Take a few moments at regular points each day to calm your breathing, and try some of the following ways to anchor yourself and remind yourself that right now, focusing on getting better is the only thing you need to be doing.

1. **When you first wake up, take a few minutes to sit in silence.** I do this every day, even when I'm feeling well. I make myself a cup of herbal tea and before I've looked at my phone or turned on the radio, I give myself a moment of reflection, calm, and headspace before the day properly begins.

2. **Do a simple meditation body scan.** Starting from the top of your head and going right down to your fingers and toes, tune into each part of your body and notice any sensations you can feel. Slow your breathing, and if your mind wanders, bring it back to your body. This is also a great mindfulness technique if you feel out of your head or are anxious. I do this a lot with my son, who suffers from anxiety.

3. **Counting and breathing.** It sounds too simple, but counting in your head while breathing calmly is a really effective way to take your focus away from feeling unwell. This is especially helpful if you are in the throes of nausea, have a fever, or are experiencing pain. Every time you become distracted, start counting from one again. There's no need to do any fancy breathing here, just breathe deeply and calmly.

4. **Three things.** This is a popular anchoring technique for anxiety, and I find it useful in periods of ill health too. Sit or lie down comfortably and name three things you can see, feel, and hear.

5. **Two questions.** Ask yourself these two questions: How do I feel? What do I need? Listen to your instant responses. This will help you focus on the most pressing issues in your body and/or mind. Gut instinct and your intuition are normally right, so always trust yourself.

6. **Reflect.** At the end of the day (always when I am cozy in bed), I take a few minutes to reflect on the day and how it has been. If you keep a journal, this is a great time to write in it. Otherwise, simply spend a few minutes reflecting in your head. This can also help you see the progress you're making on your path to recovery.

Gentle

Be kind to yourself as you recuperate and stay mindful of your mental health. We often experience poor sleep through illness, worrying, and generally not feeling our best and this, along with our symptoms, can leave us feeling a little vulnerable and more emotional than usual. The language you use about yourself at this time is so important. It can be hard to spend so much time inside your own head, so if you find any negativity creeping in, imagine you're speaking to a friend in your position. What would you say? You'd be reassuring and supportive, so treat yourself the same way too.

This section is all about finding ways to practice self-compassion—from getting in as much rest as you can to soothing recipes that will comfort and restore. I know recovery can feel relentless and repetitive at times, and it can sometimes feel as though life is passing you by while you're stuck inside. But remind yourself that everything will be there when you're feeling better again, and that stressing about it won't help you to heal.

Try repeating some of the healing mantras opposite to keep you focused on getting better and lift your mood.

HEALING WORDS

You will come back stronger
than before.

Every phase of life has something
to teach us.

Nothing stays the same for ever.

Illness is not weakness.

All I need to do today is this.

I am healing.

I trust in my body's ability to
get better.

I will take one day at a time.

I will accept what I cannot control.

Better rest

Sleep is often elusive when we're stressed out or unwell, and fretting about not sleeping can make the whole thing worse. Illnesses don't just stop at night, so don't worry if your sleep becomes a bit erratic while you're ill or in a period of recovery. Rest whenever you can as sleep is an amazing healer, even if that means naps on the sofa or going back to bed for a bit during the day. That said, once you're starting to feel a little better, establishing a bit of your regular routine—perhaps showering, eating breakfast, and putting on clean clothes—can help you feel a bit more like yourself. As well as the ways we all know about—creating a calm sleeping environment, no caffeine, and no screens—here are my top tips to aid rest and sleep, especially when you're going through a period of ill health.

Vitamin and nutrient top-off. If we lack magnesium and vitamin C, this can cause disruptions to our sleep. You can find magnesium in nuts, seeds, and oats. If you're feeling up to it, try the oatmeal recipes on pages 72–73. They make a great soothing supper too.

Get a good bedtime routine. Even if you've been in bed for much of the day, a bedtime routine can signal to your body and mind that it's time to rest. I find it really helps me get a better night's sleep—I go to town with a relaxing bath, maybe some Epsom salts, and/or some sleepy bedtime oil, dim lights, and a mug of herbal tea.

Calm a racing mind. If you know there's something specific bothering you that's going to keep you wired and awake, write it down or talk it over before bed to help ease your worries. Then reflect on your day and make a list of three things that were good. They can be as small as eating a healthy meal or having a rejuvenating shower. Let's all take time to appreciate the small things more.

CBD and reishi mushrooms. I swear by these to help with deeper sleep. I use a few drops of CBD oil at night under my tongue before bed and it makes me feel really calm. I also have a few drops in the morning, often added to a juice or smoothie, if I am feeling stressed out or anxious. I usually make a tea using powdered medicinal mushrooms and hot water. See pages 109–11 for more on medicinal mushrooms.

Yoga nidra or yogic sleep. This is an incredibly powerful guided meditation that takes you into a deep state of relaxation, somewhere between being asleep and being awake. It's an amazing way to feel rested if you've had a bad night's sleep.

Find moments to relax during the day. It sounds obvious, but if you've been unable to sleep properly at night, take it easy when you can during the day—watch a film, do some simple stretches, or find some activities that are soothing and relaxing, such as watering your plants or trimming off their dead leaves. Take a nap if you can, but if you can't, close your eyes and do the body scan on page 35 or the breathing exercises on pages 47–48.

The seven types of rest we need. According to Dr. Saundra Dalton-Smith, these are physical, mental, spiritual, emotional, social, sensory, and creative. Identify how you can rest in each of these ways during the day or across the week. Tap into your emotions to work out which type of rest you're craving.

Include some physical activity in your day. This can be a tough one when you're unwell, but even if you are in the hospital you're encouraged to get out of bed if you can and do some stretches, go for a short walk, and generally get the blood flowing and the muscles working. Don't overdo it, but build up slowly. Keeping active can really help in your recovery.

The right temperature. Keeping your room at a suitable temperature makes such a difference. Since reaching my forties, I get hot flashes at night, so keeping the room coolish and wearing the right pj's helps me sleep better. There's nothing worse than waking up in a sweat. A little fresh air can help too—leave the window open to keep the air circulating.

A warm shower or bath before bed. As well as being relaxing, there's also science behind this one! As you go to sleep, your body temperature cools, so having a warm shower or bath before bed helps mimic this and can help send you off to sleep more easily.

Don't panic. If you do wake up in the night, don't start worrying about it. Try one of the calming techniques on page 35, and if you still can't fall back to sleep, get up and change location. Read a book (avoid your phone or other screens), have a small snack or a warm drink, and head back to bed when you feel sleepy.

Simple healing broth
+ ramen noodles

This is my ultimate go-to comfort soup that I make whenever I've been ill or am just feeling a bit low and out of sorts. It instantly makes me feel better—and is so simple to make. Miso is full of probiotics to give your gut health a helping hand if you've been experiencing nausea or digestive issues, and if you've been sweating out a fever, the saltiness will help replace those lost electrolytes. If your appetite isn't quite there yet, leave out the noodles, tofu, and spinach; the simple light broth will help soothe your stressed-out system.

1 tbsp miso paste
  (I like white miso)
1 garlic clove, chopped
1 tsp toasted sesame
  oil (or any other oil
  will do)
3½ ounces mushrooms,
  washed and sliced
  (I like shiitake)
3 carrots, sliced
2 heads of bok choy,
  chopped
2 scallions, chopped
2 tbsp soy sauce or
  tamari
4 cups water

Optional:
2 x 3-ounce packs of
  dried ramen noodles
1¾ ounces spinach,
  washed and sliced
1¾ ounces tofu, cubed

Mix the miso paste with a little hot water until dissolved. Set aside.

Sauté the garlic in the oil in a pan over medium heat for about 2 minutes or until soft.

Add the mushrooms, carrots, bok choy, scallions, and soy sauce to the pan. Cook for about 5 minutes or until soft.

Add the water and bring to a boil.

If you are having noodles, add them now and cook as directed on the package. Add the spinach and tofu at this point too, if using. Serve hot.

Flu-buster golden turmeric soup + brown rice

When flu season comes around, this nourishing, restorative soup will help get you back to recovery. Ginger and turmeric give it a zing and help fight infection, and brown rice and potatoes are a gentle way to get some extra energy in if you're feeling wiped out. If you haven't been able to eat much, try a small portion to tempt your appetite—it's easy on your digestion and full of so much veggie goodness.

2 tbsp olive oil
1-inch piece fresh
  turmeric, peeled and
  finely chopped (or
  1 tsp ground)
1-inch piece fresh
  ginger, peeled and
  finely chopped
a handful of fresh
  parsley, roughly
  chopped
1 tsp mixed dried herbs
1 celery stalk, diced
1 medium carrot, diced
4 cups veggie stock
¾ cup brown rice (I like
  to use brown basmati),
  rinsed and drained
1 large potato, washed,
  peeled, and diced
1 bay leaf
1 cup frozen peas
salt and pepper

Add the oil to a large pan and warm over medium heat.

Add the turmeric and ginger, the fresh parsley and mixed herbs, the celery, and the carrot, and cook slowly for 10 minutes over medium heat.

Add the stock, brown rice, potato, and bay leaf. Bring to a boil. Cover and lower the heat, then simmer for 30 minutes, adding the peas for the last 10 minutes. Season to taste with salt and pepper and add more water if you need to or prefer a lighter soup. Serve with optional toppings if you like.

Optional toppings:
chopped fresh parsley
seeds (also see
  Toasted nuts or seeds
  recipe on page 19)
thinly sliced raw kale
coconut yogurt

HEALING HYDRATION

Keeping hydrated when you're sick is one of the very best—and easiest—ways you can support your immune system (see pages 20–21). Hot drinks are especially soothing if you have cold or flu symptoms, like a sore throat or a stuffy nose—they feel like a big hug in a mug.

Here are the four drinks I make all the time at home as they help solve the most common complaints, from colds and nausea to PMS. If you're stuck in bed, brew a batch and keep it in an insulated mug to sip on whenever you need it.

ALL SERVE 2

Spiced saffron tea
—
For low mood, PMS, and acne outbreaks.
—
Prep time: 10 minutes

2 cups water
1 tbsp sugar
5 saffron strands
1 cinnamon stick
1-inch piece fresh ginger, peeled and grated
1 lemon, quartered
10 to 12 fresh mint leaves

· Brew all the ingredients in a teapot for at least 10 minutes and enjoy.

Honey + ginger steamer
—
For sore throats and coughs.
—
Prep time: 20 minutes

1 lemon
4 cups water
5 ounces fresh ginger, peeled and cut into 1-inch pieces
2 tbsp honey

· Cut the lemon in half, squeeze its juice into a cup, and set the juice aside. Cut the squeezed lemon into quarters and add to a medium pan with the water and ginger.

· Bring to a boil over high heat, then reduce the heat to low and simmer for 20 minutes.

· Carefully strain the tea through a fine-mesh sieve to remove the ginger and lemon. Stir in the reserved lemon juice and the honey.

Medicine-ball tea

—

For colds and flu.

—

Prep time: 10 minutes

¾ cup water
¾ cup lemonade (any type)
1 mint tea bag
1 tbsp honey
1 drop peppermint extract (optional)
lemon slices, to serve

· Bring the water and lemonade to a
  simmer in a small pan. Remove from
  the heat and add the tea bag. Cover
  and steep for 3 minutes.

· Discard the tea bag, add the honey,
  and stir until dissolved. Add the
  peppermint extract if desired.
  Divide the tea between two mugs
  and serve immediately with a thin
  slice of lemon.

Three-minute ginger-aid

—

For nausea and sickness (an excellent
hangover cure too!).

—

Prep time: 10 minutes

9 ounces fresh ginger, washed,
  peeled, and chopped
1½ cups boiling water
5 or 6 limes
½ cup honey
1½ cups soda water

· Add the ginger to a teapot, then
  pour the water over the ginger in
  the teapot as if you were making
  tea. Let it brew for 10 minutes.

· While the ginger tea is brewing,
  cut the limes in half and juice them,
  using a citrus juicer or the back of
  a fork, into a pitcher.

· Pour the ginger tea through a sieve
  into the pitcher with the lime juice.
  Next add the honey and stir until
  dissolved. Chill in the fridge. Serve
  topped with the soda water.

Breathe

When we're stressed out, in pain or feeling unwell, our breathing often becomes shallow, panicky, high in our chests, and quicker than usual. This doesn't help reassure our body and mind that everything is OK. Fast breathing activates the fight-or-flight response, sending our body into panic mode. It's deep, slow, restorative belly breathing that we need in order to calm our systems, and to protect and boost our immunity.

Breathing fully and deeply activates the parasympathetic nervous system. This is sometimes known as the "rest and digest" state, and it is where we need to be in order to heal, detoxify, and repair. In this state, our heart rate lowers, we feel more relaxed, and our body can get on with all the processes it needs to do on a daily basis—including recovering from illness. A properly functioning parasympathetic nervous system increases the oxygen circulating in our body, improves digestion, helps you sleep better, eases anxiety and depression, helps eliminate toxins by regulating the lymphatic system, and gives you more energy. Sadly, in our busy, always-on modern lives, most of us find ourselves frequently in the opposite state, the sympathetic state—the high-alert, running-from-bears state, which means our heart rate is up, muscles are tense, and we constantly feel a bit wired. If you spend long enough in this state, it can lead to all kinds of digestive, sleep, and emotional issues—and more. We need both states to work together, but we definitely shouldn't be constantly feeling like we're being chased by a bear . . .

There are lots of ways to bring ourselves back into the parasympathetic state, including eating well, reducing caffeine and sugar, creating more downtime, focusing on getting better rest and sleep (see pages 38–39), gentle exercise (see pages 80–81), meditation, and breathwork.

The power of breathwork is a bit of a hot topic in wellness circles, but it's not a new idea at all. The positive effects of breathing properly have been practiced for thousands of years across many cultures. The most common place you'll find a focus on breathing is in yoga. Unlike our impression of yoga from social media, its main focus is not on stretches, balance, and doing headstands.

It's on regulating the breath. In yogic tradition, it is believed that our breath carries our life force and that proper breathing can help us live longer.

Finding time in our day to focus on our breathing also creates some much-needed headspace to reflect, rest, and restore. See the following page for a deep-breathing technique to get you started and an immunity-boosting breathwork.

Also see pages 148–9 for information on adaptogens and how they can help manage your stress response, and page 147 for how cold-water therapy (in the form of a cold shower) can help stimulate the parasympathetic nervous system.

How to breathe properly

Breathing properly and deeply is incredibly powerful. Try this in bed before you get up or go to sleep, or at any point during the day when you feel you need to calm your nervous system.

1. Sit or lie comfortably. Close your eyes if it helps you focus. Place one hand on your tummy and one hand on your chest.

2. Breathe calmly and deeply in through your nose. Your tummy should rise up as you breathe in, and lower as you breathe out through your nose. This is your diaphragm contracting, allowing more air into your lungs. Your chest shouldn't move much, and you definitely shouldn't be raising your shoulders—if you feel your shoulders moving, lower them down and push them back.

3. Start to slow down your breathing and count your breaths. Your out-breath should be longer than your in-breath. Imagine traveling along the edges of a window or door as you breathe. Your in-breath should be on the shorter sides, and the out-breath along the longer sides, and there should be a small pause at the top and bottom of each breath.

4. Try this for a couple of minutes, building up to 10 or more minutes whenever you need to find some balance. It's amazing how different you'll feel even after this short amount of time.

IMMUNITY-BOOSTING BREATHWORK: DOG BREATHING

This is basically panting like a dog and is thought to help the body eliminate toxins and increase the amount of oxygen circulating in the body. Don't try this if you are pregnant, and stop for a break if you start to feel light-headed.

1. Sit comfortably on the floor, cross-legged, or in a chair with your feet flat on the ground. Keep your back straight, chest out, and lower your shoulders back and down.

2. Stick your tongue out as far as it will go and breathe quickly through your mouth—panting like a dog. You should feel your stomach muscles really engage as you breathe—it's a good workout for them too. Breathe like this for 20 seconds, building yourself up over time to 5 minutes.

3. Finish by breathing deeply and slowly for 1 minute, and then have a big glass of water.

Tummy-loving simple stew

Our digestion can often take a hit when we've been sick. This gentle, nourishing stew is creamy from the beans, sweet potato, and coconut milk and is high in fiber to help get things back on track. If you're feeling weak or having difficulty concentrating, the folate boost can help ease lingering symptoms. Serve as is or with a hunk of fresh bread.

2 tbsp olive oil
2 large leeks, washed
  and sliced
1 carrot, chopped
1 celery stalk, chopped
3 garlic cloves,
  chopped
3 large sweet
  potatoes, chopped
  into small chunks
1¼ cups veggie stock
14-ounce can
  cannellini beans
14-ounce can butter
  beans
14-ounce can chopped
  tomatoes
13½-ounce can
  coconut milk
zest and juice of
  1 lemon
1 tsp soy sauce or
  tamari
salt and pepper
fresh parsley, to serve

Heat the oil in a large pan.

Add the leeks, carrot, and celery and fry for 2 to 3 minutes until soft. Add the garlic, sweet potatoes, and a good pinch of salt and mix well. Cook for another 2 minutes, then add the veggie stock and simmer for 5 minutes. Put the lid on and leave for 10 minutes, stirring occasionally.

Once the sweet potatoes are soft and cooked, add the beans, chopped tomatoes, and coconut milk and stir well.

Taste and adjust the seasoning to how you like it. Add the lemon zest and juice, soy sauce, and fresh parsley. Enjoy!

Calming green soup

This soup does exactly what it says on the can! Vibrantly colored and packed with nutrition, this chunky green veg soup is rich in magnesium, calcium, iron, and vitamin K to help fight fatigue, PMS, period pains and headaches, and can soothe a busy mind. The color green has been shown in countless studies to reduce stress and calm anxiety, most likely because of its presence in nature, so sit down and enjoy the restorative powers of this bowl of green goodness.

1 tbsp coconut oil
1 leek, washed and chopped
1 zucchini, washed and chopped
1 head broccoli, washed and chopped
3 garlic cloves, chopped
a handful of fresh parsley, chopped
a handful of fresh cilantro, chopped
2 cups veggie stock
1 bay leaf
3½ ounces kale or other greens, washed and sliced
3½ ounces spinach, washed and sliced
a pinch of salt
1 tsp soy sauce or tamari
juice of 1 lemon

Heat the oil in a large pan and sauté the leek, zucchini and broccoli with the garlic and fresh herbs for about 3 minutes.

Add the stock and bay leaf. Then add the kale or greens, put the lid on, and cook for 20 minutes over low heat.

Finally, stir in the spinach, salt, soy sauce or tamari, and lemon juice and serve.

Steamed kitchari

Kitchari is a traditional Ayurvedic dish made from lentils and rice. It's usually eaten at breakfast, but I think it's good any time of day. Easy to digest, with lots of soothing, healing spices, it can give your digestive system a bit of a break, while still containing complete proteins and a good level of carbs to keep your blood sugar levels in balance. Some people even believe kitchari can help remove toxins from the body. Either way, it's delicious, simple to make and is a great way to support your immune system while you recover from a period of illness.

1 cup dried yellow split peas or lentils
¼ cup long-grain brown rice
3 tbsp coconut oil
1-inch piece fresh ginger, peeled and grated
2 tsp ground cumin
1 tsp ground coriander
1 tsp fennel seeds
1 tsp ground fenugreek
1 tsp ground turmeric
a pinch of salt
4 cups veggie stock
1 small head of broccoli, finely chopped into an almost ricelike texture (about 3 cups total)
1 medium zucchini, coarsely grated (about 1 cup)
1 ounce baby spinach, roughly chopped
a handful of cilantro leaves
coconut yogurt, to serve (optional)

Rinse the yellow split peas or lentils and rice in a sieve until the water runs clear.

Put a large pan over medium heat, heat the coconut oil, then add the ginger and spices and cook for a few minutes.

Add the lentils and rice and stir to coat in the spices. Add the salt and pour in the vegetable stock. Bring to a boil, cover, and reduce the heat to medium-low. Simmer for 35 to 45 minutes, stirring occasionally, until the lentils are tender but not mushy and most of the liquid has been absorbed. (You may need to add more water if the mixture becomes too dry or begins to stick to the bottom of the pan.)

Stir in the broccoli. Cover and cook for another 4 to 5 minutes. Stir in the zucchini and spinach, then remove from the heat and let stand for 5 minutes. Serve warm, topped with the cilantro and a dollop of yogurt, if desired.

CHAPTER 2

Replenish

Immunity-recharging smoothies 62

Super nourish berry + beet • Hydrating pineapple + turmeric • Mood-boosting date + vanilla • Citrus zing

Vitamin C supercharged creamy squash + pepper soup 64

Comforting savory crumble 66

Upside-down pineapple cake 68

Oatmeal + toppers 72

Banana + cinnamon • Tahini, date + toasted almond • Yogurt + berries • Ginger + pear • Spiced oats + caramelized banana

Chickpea chowder 74

Slow-cooked comfort stew with barley + all the veggies 76

Tomato, kale + butter bean hotpot 78

Sweet potato + black bean feast 84

Roasted cauliflower tacos + zingy ginger salsa + avocado 86

Turmeric, ginger + citrus muffins 91

Replenish

This chapter is all about big, powerful nutrition boosters! By now, hopefully you're coming out the other side of whatever had you not feeling your best, and it's the perfect time to think about replacing those key vitamins and nutrients you may have lost by not eating properly while you weren't feeling well. These are the recipes to encourage your appetite back, help you feel more energized, and lift your mood. They focus on maximizing your intake of colorful fruits, veg, beans and legumes, and grains while still being gentle on your digestion. On pages 59–61 I've also listed the most important vitamins, minerals, and nutrients to try to include in your diet in the post-recovery phase; have a look and see what you feel you're missing so you can mix-and-match your own mealtimes too. Or if you need an instant hit of nutrition, try one of my supercharged smoothies on page 63.

It's so important not to rush things, though. Stay aware of your energy levels and keep tuning in to what your body is telling you. If you need to rest or take a break, do it! Listen to what your body is telling you. Be kind to yourself as you build yourself back up to full strength and don't overdo things.

On the following pages, you'll find some of my favorite ways to boost my mood—because replenishing yourself after illness is also about feeling mentally strong again. Feeling unwell is hard work and can often leave us experiencing low moods, especially if it's been going on awhile, so try to find ways to give yourself a little lift throughout the day and create some positivity. It can be helpful to focus on some of the activities or people you want to include more of in your life once you are well again, to help keep you motivated as you continue to recover— but please don't put any pressure on yourself. And, as always, if you find yourself feeling really out of sorts for a longer period of time, check in with your GP.

FOCUS ON WHAT'S IMPORTANT

When we're ill or are otherwise forced to take time out, many people find it can result in a bit of a shift in our priorities.

Maybe we realize we've been working too hard or spending too much of our time devoted to activities that aren't making us happy anymore. Our world becomes naturally smaller while we attend to our recovery, and the things we miss most, that we want to do more of when we're better, and the people we want to prioritize, are our mind's way of telling us what's truly important to us. Maybe you want to reconnect with someone from your past, or get a dog, or finally leave a job you hate . . . Although getting back out there may still feel a challenge or a long way off right now, it can be helpful and motivating to use this time to have a think about whether there's anything you want to do differently when you're well again. Or perhaps your life will be permanently changed as you learn to manage an ongoing condition or mitigate a relapse, in which case building a world that looks a little different from before, but that is based around what brings you the most joy and support, is going to be key to your ongoing wellness journey.

Nourish

I truly believe that taking the time to make and eat a nourishing meal is the ultimate act in self-care. It's the reason I started my Nourish Packages—I wanted to share the healing power of plant-based nutrition and enable people to taste a little bit of the love I put into all my home-cooked meals. Thinking about what we're going to eat shows that we believe we deserve to be looked after, and I find that preparing even very simple meals can be a soothing, creative process that heals and nourishes my mind, at the same time as providing me with a big boost of goodness.

Colorful, flavorful food, like the recipes in this chapter, will help nourish you mentally as well as physically. As you make these recipes, I hope you feel comforted and reassured, and know that you're filling your body with the nutrition it needs to feel better. If you're not properly nourished—and that includes nourishing all parts of yourself, including your mental well-being—you can't be the best version of yourself. So, take the time to think about what you're going to eat, and what your body and mind need to feel happy, and consider it an important step in your healing process.

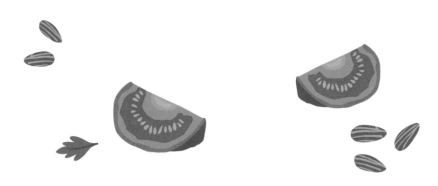

Key vitamins and nutrients for post-recovery (and where to find them)

Get yourself back on track following a period of illness and boost your immunity by focusing on including as many nutrient-dense foods in your diet as you can. Use this list to help maximize your mealtimes, snacks and drinks to give your body and mind everything they need to start feeling their best again. These all contain powerful immunity-protection properties, so I try to make sure I cover a variety across the week to see optimum benefits.

Healthy fats
Healthy fats are vital for good health. They help with muscle growth, reduce inflammation, regulate blood sugars, support your brain and heart, and can even improve your mood. If you have been feeling unwell, it's really important to make sure you are eating enough healthy fats. Aim to include a good balance of omega-3s, -6s, and -9s in your diet. Good sources include avocado, nuts, hemp, pumpkin and sunflower seeds, dark chocolate, walnuts, olive and coconut oils, and seaweed.

Iodine
Many people are iodine deficient. A lack of it is linked to low energy, frequent infections, and even feeling the cold more. It also plays a key role in supporting our thyroid. It's not easy to source from our diets but plant-based sources include fortified milks, whole grains, kale, potatoes with their skin, and seaweed.

Iron
Iron is vital for helping our red blood cells transport oxygen around our body and to support our immune system, and iron deficiency (anemia) can leave us feeling exhausted, cold, and with poor focus and attention. Find iron in tofu, beans and legumes, dark leafy greens, nuts, and seeds.

Magnesium
The ultimate destressing mineral, it can relax our muscles and soothe an anxious mind to aid better sleep. It also supports good heart health as well as contributing to many other functions in the body. Nuts and seeds are fantastic sources, especially chia seeds, pumpkin seeds, and almonds. You can also find it in oats.

Potassium

Weakness and fatigue can be a sign you're not getting enough potassium. Boost your intake from bananas, leafy greens, broccoli, dried fruit, beans, and lentils.

Probiotics and prebiotics

These support your gut health and are especially important if you've been taking antibiotics or have had any digestive issues. My Funky ferments on pages 102–103 are an amazing source of both—also see page 100 for more on the importance of gut health.

Protein

It's important to ensure you are eating enough protein post-recovery to help regain muscle strength and any weight you might have lost when you were unwell.

Protein powders (added to smoothies, energy balls, oatmeal, or overnight oats) can be an easy way to boost your protein levels, especially if your appetite isn't quite there yet. Stay away from whey protein as it can cause stomach cramps and digestion issues (whey is also a by-product of the dairy industry). Plant-based foods that are high in protein include beans and legumes, tofu, quinoa, and nuts.

Selenium

An antioxidant with incredible immunity-supporting powers, we are often low in selenium following illness. Boost your intake with grains, barley, nuts, and seeds—see my Slow-cooked comfort stew with barley + all the veggies on page 76.

Vitamin B12

This vital B vitamin is essential for so many functions in the body, from creating red blood cells to keeping your nerve cells healthy, and is thought to protect the brain too. It can mainly be found in animal products, so if you're eating a plant-based diet, it's important to make sure you're consuming adequate amounts either through a supplement or my favorite source, Marmite! Try the Marmite + mushroom + avocado toast on page 29. Otherwise, fortified milk and seaweed are great ways to up your intake.

Vitamin C

Providing all-around support for your immune system, this antioxidant also helps build and repair bone, muscles, and other tissues in the body. Citrus fruits are high in vitamin C, as are peppers, kiwis, pineapples, tomatoes, watercress, and mangoes.

Vitamin D

Otherwise known as the sunshine vitamin. Children and adults are advised to take a vitamin D supplement throughout the winter months. Vitamin D helps the absorption of calcium in the body, is essential for bone health, and also supports immunity. A deficiency can leave you feeling tired and weak. Plant-based sources include mushrooms and fortified milk.

Zinc

Vital for cell growth and repair and an amazing immunity-boosting mineral. Find it in beans and legumes (try my Easy hummus on page 15), nuts, and seeds.

IMMUNITY-RECHARGING SMOOTHIES

Fruits and green leafy veg blended up into smoothies are a brilliant and quick way to give yourself an extra boost of vitamins, minerals, and fiber. If you've been unwell but are starting to feel a bit better, now's the perfect time to consider what might have been missing from your diet if you haven't been eating properly, or to give yourself an extra helping hand to get back to your best. Try these colorful, uplifting, and nourishing smoothies to replenish your reserves and provide some much-needed feel-good nutrition. Have a go at making your own too: see pages 59–61 for my list of key vitamins and minerals to add to your diet post-illness and where to find them, so that you can mix and match ingredients depending on what your body is telling you it needs. There's no need to spend a fortune on fresh produce either: frozen fruits and veg are much cheaper and contain just as much goodness.

I often also add extra plant protein, plant and fruit powders, medicinal mushrooms, and superfood powders to my smoothies, along with nuts and/or chia seeds to supercharge their healing properties. Read about medicinal mushrooms and why I love them so much on pages 109–111 and about plant and superfood powders on pages 170–171.

ALL SERVE 2 | *Prep time: 5 minutes*

Blend all the ingredients for each smoothie on high in a regular blender until smooth.

Super nourish berry + beet

—

vitamin D (kale), vitamin C (kale and berries), iron (beet), iodine (pineapple), zinc (kale)

—

Banish lingering cold and flu symptoms. Can also ease nausea and sickness.

2½ ounces kale, washed
1 small beet, washed, peeled, and chopped
½ cup water
½ orange, peeled
1 cup frozen mixed berries
3½ ounces frozen pineapple
½-inch piece fresh ginger, peeled and chopped
1 tsp coconut oil
a handful of ice

Hydrating pineapple + turmeric

—

vitamin C (limes), magnesium (coconut water), iron (pineapple), vitamin B12 (banana)

—

Immunity-boosting and anti-inflammatory, with coconut water for rehydration after a fever or tummy bug.

¾ cup frozen pineapple
1 medium banana
juice of 2 limes
1 tbsp coconut oil
1 tsp ground turmeric
½ cup coconut water
1 cup water
a handful of ice

Mood-boosting date + vanilla

—

magnesium and iron (dates), probiotics (coconut yogurt), vitamin C and magnesium (bananas), zinc (almond milk)

—

For when you're feeling weak and tired. Also calms anxiety and boosts low mood.

10 large dates, pitted
½ cup coconut yogurt
1 banana, frozen
1 cup almond milk
1 tbsp honey or maple syrup
½ tsp vanilla extract
1 tbsp peanut butter
½ tsp ground cinnamon
a good pinch of salt
a handful of ice
Toasted nuts or seeds (page 19), to scatter over the top

Citrus zing

—

vitamin C (oranges), vitamin B12 (oranges and bananas), vitamin D (mango), magnesium (almonds)

—

All-around immunity boost, especially for colds and flu.

3 oranges, peeled
1 large banana, frozen if possible
1 cup frozen mango chunks
1 cup almond or coconut milk
1 cup coconut yogurt
a few strands of saffron (optional)

Vitamin C supercharged creamy squash + pepper soup

Just looking at this soup will make you feel instantly more positive. Bright orange squash and fiery red peppers with creamy coconut milk and gently warming spices—it's like a glowing sunny day in a bowl. Overflowing with vitamin C, it will also help kick any cold and flu symptoms that are hanging around and give your immune system a boost.

―――――

1 medium butternut
   squash, cut in half
   and seeded
2 red bell peppers
2½ cups veggie stock
13½-ounce can
   coconut milk
1-inch piece fresh
   ginger, peeled and
   grated
2 garlic cloves,
   chopped
1 tsp ground cumin
salt and pepper

Optional toppings:
a drizzle of olive oil
chopped fresh parsley
freshly ground black
   pepper
toasted nuts and/or
   seeds
crème fraîche or yogurt

Preheat the oven to 375°F on the convection setting. Line a baking sheet with baking paper, put the squash flesh-side down, and roast for 25 minutes. Add the bell peppers and roast for about 25 more minutes. Let cool for about 5 minutes.

Remove the stem and seeds from the peppers. Using a spoon, scoop out the flesh of the squash from the skin.

Reserve a few pieces of the squash for garnish, if you like, then add the remaining squash, the peppers, veggie stock, coconut milk, ginger, garlic, cumin, and salt and black pepper to taste to a blender. Transfer to a pan and warm over low heat until hot and ready to serve. Blend until smooth and add any extra toppings.

Comforting savory crumble

Crumble topping:
1½ cups plus 2 tbsp
 jumbo oats
⅓ cup chickpea flour
 (or all-purpose flour)
¼ cup chopped walnuts
2 tbsp hulled hemp
 seeds
1 tsp garlic powder
1 tsp herbes de Provence
1 tbsp nutritional yeast
salt and pepper
⅓ cup plus 2 tbsp
 olive oil

Filling:
1 sweet potato, peeled
 and cut into ½-inch
 pieces
½ small head of
 cauliflower, cut into
 florets
2 medium carrots, cut
 into ¼-inch pieces
2 medium red onions,
 sliced
2 cooked medium
 beets, diced
10 cherry tomatoes,
 halved
2 garlic cloves,
 chopped
1 tsp English mustard
½ cup vegan crème
 fraîche (or cream)
2 tbsp olive oil
salt and pepper
2 tsp dried thyme
a handful of fresh
 parsley, minced

Savory crumble was one of the first recipes I learned to cook when I was about eight years old—and I have been obsessed with it ever since! Sweet potato, cauliflower, and carrots are hearty and satisfying and provide a really good range of nutrition, but it's a great way to use up any veg you have—mixed root veg work really well too. The walnuts and hemp seeds on top make it crunchy and delicious, adding an extra boost of nutrients.

To make the crumble topping, put the oats, flour, nuts and seeds, garlic powder, herbs, nutritional yeast, and salt and pepper to taste in a large bowl. Mix in the olive oil and then rub together with your hands until it looks like a crumble mixture. Set aside.

Preheat the oven to 350°F on the convection setting. Grease a large baking dish and set aside.

To prepare the filling, put all the veggies along with the garlic, mustard, crème fraîche, olive oil, salt, pepper, thyme, and parsley in a large bowl. Mix until well combined, then put into the prepared baking dish. Sprinkle the crumble over the veggies and bake for about 45 minutes.

Serve with a fresh and crunchy green salad.

Upside-down pineapple cake

Replenishing your reserves isn't all about vitamins—it's also about making you feel good again too! And oh my goodness, this cake will make everyone happy. It's delicious on its own, served warm, or with custard.

For the topping:
3½ tbsp vegan butter, melted
½ cup Demerara sugar
15-ounce can pineapple slices (keep the juice for the cake)

For the cake:
1¾ cups all-purpose flour
scant 1 cup Demerara sugar
1 tsp baking soda
½ tsp salt
½ cup plus 2 tbsp plant-based milk
¼ cup pineapple juice (saved from the can)
1 tsp vanilla extract
⅓ cup unrefined coconut oil, melted
1 tbsp apple cider vinegar

Preheat the oven to 350°F on the convection setting and grease a 9-inch round cake pan with coconut oil or vegan butter.

Melt the vegan butter, pour it into the bottom of the cake pan, and spread it around so it forms an even layer. Sprinkle the brown sugar evenly over the melted butter and then lay the pineapple slices on the bottom of the pan in a single layer. Set aside while you make the cake batter.

Sift the flour into a mixing bowl, add the sugar, baking soda, and salt and mix well. Then add the milk, pineapple juice, vanilla, melted coconut oil, and vinegar and mix well. (I use a handheld mixer.)

Pour the cake mixture over the pineapple. Place on the middle rack of the oven and bake for 50 minutes.

Let the cake cool for at least 15 minutes before taking it out of the pan. The syrup should drizzle down the sides.

Uplift

Studies have shown that having an optimistic and sunny outlook is one of the best ways we can strengthen and support our immunity in the long term. But when we're coming out of a period of ill health, our mood can sometimes take a while to catch up. Give it a helping hand by identifying ways you can introduce as many small moments of joy into your day as possible. These are not big-ticket plans, but micro-moments of pleasure that quickly add up to a more joyful approach to life in general. From waking up to bedtime, sprinkle your day with uplifting activities that make you smile. Here are some ideas.

Start your day with a soothing, warm drink in your favorite mug. See page 44 for hot drink inspiration.

Shower using your favorite products. Try my Glow-up shower scrub (opposite) for an instant lift, or have a long soak in the bath with your favorite bath oil or some Epsom salts and the window open to feel the breeze. I use a dry body brush before showering to get my circulation going and help stimulate the lymphatic system—it's also a great exfoliator!

Wear bright colors. Keep cozy and comfortable and banish dull wardrobes. Putting on red lipstick and jewelry is a classic but reliable way to make you feel a bit special—especially if you've mostly been wearing sweatpants or pj's if you've been unwell.

Mood lighting. Are your lamps too bright or too dim? Adjust the lighting to create a cozy vibe or shift up a notch for a more vibrant energy.

A new picture for your wall. Find something that brings you joy every time you look at it, frame it, and hang it up so you can see it throughout the day. It doesn't have to be expensive—a postcard with an uplifting message or a photo of good times is perfect.

Have a good clean-out. It may not seem like a way to get instant joy, but it's such a great feeling when you make space by clearing your clutter, sorting out your wardrobe and getting rid of things you no longer want or need, either by selling them online or by giving them to charity. It'll really lift your mood and make you feel productive!

Sort your pantry out. Do it at your leisure and only if you have the strength. Get rid of anything that is out of date or that you do not use—give it to a local food bank or use a food-collection app like Olio. Clean those jars and organize your spices so you know what you have and are ready to cook. Happy days!

Celebrate mealtimes. Eat your meals off pretty plates and set the table properly, even if it's lunch for one.

Call a friend. If you feel like company but aren't able to meet up IRL, call someone you know is always going to make you laugh.

Mood-boosting music. Get those feel-good tunes playing and maybe have a boogie—I guarantee you'll feel 100 per cent happier.

Go for a walk. We all know exercise is a great mood booster. Get your trainers on and get outside, whatever the weather. Try walking somewhere new. (See page 80 for more on movement.)

Give your hands a treat. I love to give my hands some love with a homemade manicure. Massage with some nice hand cream, file your nails, and put some oil on your cuticles.

Laugh out loud. Sometimes we just need a rom-com or some comedy on YouTube to lighten the mood.

Fresh bedding. There's nothing like getting between crisp, clean sheets at the end of the day.

Read a new book. I love escaping into a new book, and it's the perfect way to find enjoyment away from a screen.

Glow-up shower scrub
—

For the base:
1 cup pure cane sugar
¼ cup sweet almond oil or
  extra virgin olive oil

Optional extras:
a few drops of vitamin E oil
juice of 1 small lemon
a few drops of aromatherapy
  oil—my favorites are:
· lime for fresh/wake up
· lavender for sleepy/relax
· rosehip for dry skin
· peppermint for menopause/
  hot flashes
· clary sage for PMS/ hormone
  balance (do not use if pregnant)

Place the sugar in a small bowl and add the oil, 1 tablespoon at a time. If the mix is too oily, add a little more sugar. Add your extras and mix well. Store in a lidded container for up to 4 weeks. Use daily, massaging into wet skin and rinsing off with warm water.

OATMEAL + TOPPERS

With five kids and not a lot of money, my mom would cook huge pots of oatmeal for us almost every day during the winter months. We'd have it with sugar sprinkled on top, or maybe a bit of honey or golden syrup or chopped banana. I still love oatmeal and now cook it for my own family. Comforting and easy to digest, oats contain magnesium and melatonin, which can reduce anxiety, lift your mood, and help you get a good night's sleep—so don't just save oatmeal for breakfast! It also makes an amazing light meal at night, especially if you get in late after a long day and need something quick but nourishing.

There are so many ingredients you can top your oatmeal with for an extra nutrition boost and to make a simple bowl of oatmeal feel really decadent and special. I use all kinds of seasonal and frozen fruits, nut butters, seeds, and spices. See opposite for some of my favorite combinations.

SERVES 4 | *Prep time: 2 minutes* | *Cook time: 10 minutes*

1¾ cups oats
2½ cups milk of your
    choice (I like to use
    oat or cashew)
a pinch of salt

Place the oats and the milk in a medium pan over medium heat. Add the salt and stir with a wooden spoon. Turn the heat to low and bring to a simmer, then cook for about 5 minutes, stirring to make your oatmeal smooth and creamy. Add more milk if you like it thinner.

Serve on its own or see opposite for extra flavors and toppings.

Banana + cinnamon
—
Energy-boosting
—
Add a pinch of ground cinnamon and spoonful of maple syrup and top with sliced banana.

Tahini, date + toasted almond
—
Mood-boosting
—
Add 3 chopped pitted dates with a drizzle of tahini and then top with sliced almonds. I like to add a small pinch of salt on top, too.

Yogurt + berries
—
Immunity-boosting
—
Add a large spoonful of coconut or vanilla yogurt, plus a handful of frozen berries. Top with a handful of chopped nuts.

Ginger + pear
—
For nausea
—
Grate a ripe pear into the oats plus ½ inch of peeled fresh ginger. Stir and then add a spoonful of maple syrup on top.

Spiced oats + caramelized banana
—
For fatigue/tiredness
—
Add 1 tbsp almond butter, 1 tbsp maple syrup, 1 tsp ground cardamom, ½ tsp vanilla extract, and a pinch of salt to the oatmeal.

To make the caramelized bananas, slice 2 ripe bananas and mix with 1 tbsp maple syrup, 1 tbsp coconut oil, and 1 tbsp sesame seeds, then fry on each side until golden. Serve on top of the oatmeal with a dollop of coconut yogurt.

Chickpea chowder

Make a bowl of this creamy, silky-smooth chowder on a cold or rainy day for the ultimate self-care. It's filling and satisfying as the chickpeas and potato provide lots of great slow-release energy. Serve with thick slices of your favorite bread (try my seeded bread on page 17) to scoop up every last drop.

2 tbsp olive oil
1 onion, chopped
2 garlic cloves, chopped
2 celery stalks, chopped
1 tsp mixed herbs
4 cups veggie stock
1 large potato, peeled and chopped
4 large carrots, chopped
14-ounce can chickpeas, drained and rinsed
juice of 1 lemon
salt and pepper
a handful of fresh parsley, chopped
your favorite bread, for serving

Add the olive oil to a large pan over medium heat. Add the onion, garlic, and celery and cook for about 5 minutes until soft. Stir in the herbs and 1 cup of the veggie stock and cook for a couple more minutes.

Add the mixed herbs, stock, potato, carrots, and chickpeas, and simmer for about 20 minutes, until the potatoes and carrots are cooked.

Put half of the soup into a blender and blend until smooth. Pour the blended soup back into the pan with the unblended half and stir well.

Add the lemon juice and season with salt and pepper.

Stir in the fresh parsley and serve with a hunk of your favorite bread.

Slow-cooked comfort stew with barley + all the veggies

What I love about this dish is its simplicity. Everything goes into one big pot so it's easy to prepare, with minimal cleanup. Pearl barley is high in fiber and is a good source of selenium, a powerful antioxidant, and magnesium, which supports so many vital functions in the body. We can often be low in both after a period of illness, making pearl barley a great addition to your post-recovery mealtimes. The simply dressed spinach adds even more goodness but leave it out if you prefer. (I serve this versatile spinach side with SO many dishes—such as the Tomato, kale + butter bean hotpot on page 78 or added to my nourish bowls on pages 122–3.)

2 tbsp olive oil
1 large onion, chopped
9 ounces mushrooms, washed and sliced
2 garlic cloves, chopped
2 tbsp all-purpose flour
2 cups veggie stock
2 tbsp tomato puree
1 tbsp brown sugar
a splash of tamari or soy sauce
1 tbsp apple cider vinegar
1 bay leaf
2 sprigs thyme
⅓ cup pearl barley, rinsed and drained

3 carrots, cut into large chunks (same size as the baby potatoes)
9 ounces baby potatoes, washed

Simple spinach side (optional):
4 large handfuls of fresh spinach, washed
1 lemon
1 tbsp olive oil
1½ teaspoons apple cider vinegar
a large pinch of salt

Heat the oil in a large pan, add the onion, and fry gently for a few minutes until soft. Add the mushrooms and garlic and stir in the flour to coat everything.

Add the veggie stock, stirring to make sure no lumps remain, then add the tomato puree, brown sugar, tamari, cider vinegar, bay leaf, and thyme. Bring to a boil, then reduce the heat to maintain a simmer. Add the pearl barley, carrots, and potatoes, bring it back to a boil, and then reduce the heat again to simmer.

Simmer the stew for 30 minutes until the pearl barley, carrots, and potatoes are cooked, or transfer to a slow cooker, cover, and cook on Low for 5 hours to finish.

If you're making the spinach side, just before serving, mix all the ingredients together in a bowl until the spinach leaves are coated well.

Tomato, kale + butter bean hotpot

¼ cup olive oil, plus
  extra for drizzling
1 celery stalk, chopped
1 medium white onion,
  thinly sliced
1 large carrot, chopped
4 garlic cloves, thinly
  sliced
2 tsp smoked paprika
14-ounce can butter
  beans, drained and
  rinsed
14-ounce can
  tomatoes, chopped
a handful of fresh
  parsley, chopped
4 cups sliced chard or
  kale
4 large potatoes,
  thinly sliced into 2- to
  3-inch-long pieces
salt and pepper
zest and juice of
  1 lemon, to serve

Garlic toasts:
2 tbsp vegan butter
2 tbsp olive oil
4 garlic cloves, minced
a pinch of salt
a pinch of freshly
  ground black pepper
8 slices of bread
  (slightly stale is fine)

Every time I taste the smoky flavors in this Tomato, kale + butter bean hotpot, it takes me right back to our time living in Barcelona when the kids were small. Hearty and filling, with a gorgeous Mediterranean vibe, every spoonful reminds me of happiness and adventure. Chard is rich in iron and magnesium so is a great energy boosting ingredient, and butter beans can help encourage a slow digestive system. It'd work really well with chickpeas too.

The garlic toasts are crunchy and delicious, but if you feel these might be a bit strongly flavored for you right now, eat the hotpot on its own, or with the spinach on page 76, or whipped Seaweed butter (page 165) spread on seaweed or regular bread (see recipe on page 164).

———

Preheat the oven to 400°F on the convection setting.

Heat the oil in a large pan over medium heat. Add the celery, onion, carrot, and garlic and cook until it is all soft, about 5 minutes. Stir in the paprika, butter beans, tomatoes, and parsley, then add the greens and stir until just wilted.

Place the sliced potatoes over the top of the stew and season well with salt and pepper. Drizzle with olive oil and bake for 30 to 40 minutes until the potatoes are golden.

Meanwhile, make the garlic toasts. Mix the butter, oil, garlic, and salt and pepper in a bowl and spread evenly on both sides of the slices of bread. Fry in a skillet for about 1 minute on each side until golden.

Scatter the lemon zest and juice over the hotpot and serve.

GENTLE WAYS TO GET MOVING

As well as optimum nutrition, regular exercise is universally agreed upon as one of the best ways to enhance and support our immunity. We are not the sportiest family, but getting outside always changes the vibe, and it's so important for all of us to get away from our screens and move.

The key is to find something you enjoy doing and stick with it. You definitely don't need to go to several HIIT classes every week, turn yourself into a pretzel in yoga classes, or seek out the latest fitness trends. Something that gets your heart rate up and helps you build muscle strength is exactly what the doctor has ordered. If you can do it outside, then even better for a dose of vitamin D and some healing fresh air.

If you've been a bit immobile through illness or been stuck in bed or on the sofa, it's likely you may have lost a bit of your fitness and strength, so go slowly as you build yourself back up. It may be that even going for a gentle walk is the limit of your capabilities right now, and if so, remember that that is completely OK. Even getting out of the house can be a challenge if you've been unwell, so see every small achievement as a victory.

- The best way for our family to get moving is to head out for a good stomp with the doggy. Often our son will take his scooter when we go for a walk as it's more fun for him.

- If you're not quite up to that yet, try a gentle stroll to your local café and enjoy a comforting drink while you people-watch.

- Head to the park and sit on a bench or lie down on the grass while you listen to the birds and feel the sun on your face.

- Pack a picnic, head into nature, and look for the beauty all around you.

- We're lucky to live near the beach, so in the summer it has to be a swim or splash around in the sea. No one complains if we are going swimming as long as peanut butter sandwiches are guaranteed afterward. If you don't live near the coast, check out some wild swimming spots near you, or outdoor public pools.

- Stretch! Morning stretches are fun and so important to get the blood flowing. Gentle movements when you wake up will set you up for the rest of the day.

- I love both yoga and Pilates and don't know what I would do without my morning classes. They totally clear my head and have become almost like my therapy. As I have got older, I find gentle exercises like this are much more beneficial and enjoyable. If you can't make it to a class, there are so many amazing online videos now that you can do at home in your pj's.

Touch

Anyone that knows me will know how much I love hugs. They instantly make me feel so much better and calmer. Hugging releases serotonin and oxytocin, both powerful hormones that make us feel happy and relaxed. Hugs lower our stress levels, slow down our heart rate, reduce our blood pressure, and make us feel safe. They can also help us sleep better and heal faster. Some studies have even shown that regular hugs provide a huge boost to our immune systems so that we can fight off infections and actively avoid getting sick in the first place.

I often use simple touch techniques with my kids when they are upset or overwhelmed. I gently stroke their head or back and it soothes them almost instantly. We also have a secret handshake so they can communicate if they're feeling stressed or worried. It means they don't need to speak, which can be difficult when you are upset.

Massage (including self-massage) and acupressure, or even thick, comforting sweaters and blankets, can all produce similar effects— any kind of touch that makes you feel wrapped up, cozy, and full of love. So, whether you snuggle up with other humans or give your pets a big cuddle, don't hold back! It's scientifically proven to be good for your health.

Touch also taps into something instinctive that can often be lacking in our digital worlds. Our bodies are packed with nerve receptors and touch stimulates these receptors, and in turn our brains. It's vital we keep these networks active. That's why in this section, I've included some more interactive recipes—food to eat with your hands. They're great sharing dishes for the ultimate bonding experience.

Easy head, face and neck massage at home
—

I give myself a head, face, and neck massage at least twice a week. You can get a partner or friend to do it for you, but either way it will help produce lots of lovely oxytocin. It always cheers me up and keeps my face lovely and smooth. Spend 30 seconds to 1 minute on each stage, depending how much time you have.

1. Gently massage all over your scalp using your fingertips.

2. Reach around to the back of your neck and gently massage using sweeping motions and circular motions, avoiding massaging on any bones.

3. Wash your hands, give your face a good cleanse, and pat it dry.

4. Warm a few drops of facial oil in your hands. I make my own by using almond or argan oil as a base and adding a few drops of essential oil such as rose, rosehip, geranium, or neroli.

5. Gently massage your face with your fingertips, working across the forehead, down your nose, across your cheeks and jawbones, and up toward your ears. Use small circular movements. Using your knuckles, knead your cheeks and the side of the face.

6. Using your fingertips, smooth the frown lines down (I do this for ages!) and then smooth over the rest of the forehead.

7. Gently massage the lymph nodes—use two fingers on either side of your neck to pull down the skin very gently just above your collarbone.

8. With your fingertips, draw light half-circles under your eyes, out toward your ears.

9. End by stroking under your chin with the palms of your hands.

If you're pushed for time, use a jade roller for a quick one-minute massage. Apply light pressure and roll in an upward direction all over your clean, dry face and out toward your ears. You can do this day or night. You may want to apply a few drops of facial oil to your skin first. (Remember to wipe your jade roller afterward.)

Sweet potato + black bean feast

I call these nachos one of my "picky-picky" meals, as you can just plunk the baking sheet on the table for everyone to help themselves! It's a really simple way to encourage people to engage with what they're eating and connect with those around them. It provides so much nutritional goodness too. Black beans have an amazing nutty flavor and are packed with health benefits, from heart health to digestion. The vibrant salsa adds a zingy kick, which will make you feel alive with the joy of sharing this dish with others!

---

4 medium sweet
   potatoes, washed
   and cut into wedges
1 tbsp olive oil
1 tsp smoked paprika
1 tsp salt
2 avocados
2 limes, quartered
14-ounce can black
   beans, drained
crème fraîche or
   coconut yogurt
a bunch of cilantro,
   leaves picked and
   roughly chopped
   (reserve some for the
   salsa)
1 red onion, finely
   chopped

For the salsa:
10 cherry tomatoes
1 tbsp cilantro (from
   the bunch above)
1 garlic clove
½ small red chile
juice of 1 lime
1 tsp sugar
a pinch of salt

Preheat the oven to 425°F on the convection setting.

Put the sweet potatoes in a bowl and rub with the olive oil, smoked paprika, and salt. Then spread out on a greased baking sheet and bake for about 25 minutes until they are cooked through.

Meanwhile, make the salsa by halving the tomatoes and adding to a small bowl with the cilantro, garlic, and chopped chile. Mix the lime juice, sugar, and salt in a small bowl and then toss with the tomatoes.

Chop the avocados and toss with the lime juice.

To serve, place the sweet potatoes on a large serving tray. Scatter the black beans, avocado, and salsa on the top. Add dollops of crème fraîche, more cilantro leaves, red onion, and the lime quarters and enjoy your feast.

Roasted cauliflower tacos + zingy ginger salsa + avocado

Building your own tacos is very therapeutic. I love that everyone can create them to their exact personal preferences and really get to know the ingredients. Sharing food together like this is such a wonderful ritual and can really lift your mood if you've been feeling a bit isolated while you've been unwell. The ginger mango salsa is what elevates these simple tacos to something really special. Mango adds a color pop and burst of sweetness, and fresh ginger and all the spices will give your immune system a boost. These are also great with one or two of the Funky ferments on pages 102–3—use these instead of the Korean slaw if you like.

2 small heads
  cauliflower, cut into
  bite-size pieces
2 avocados
1 lime
8 small tortillas

Marinade:
¼ cup sunflower oil
2 tsp smoked paprika
1 tsp cayenne pepper
½ tsp ground cumin
1 tbsp tomato puree
1 tbsp maple syrup
juice of 1 lime
a pinch of salt

Ginger mango salsa:
5 ounces mango,
  peeled and chopped
1 small red onion,
  chopped
juice of 1 lime
10 fresh mint leaves
a small bunch of fresh
  cilantro
½ small red chile,
  seeded and finely
  chopped
1-inch piece fresh
  ginger, peeled and
  finely chopped
1 tsp olive oil
a pinch of salt

Korean slaw:
1 small head Chinese
  cabbage, thinly sliced
½ red cabbage, thinly
  sliced (optional)
1 medium carrot,
  grated (optional)
1 red bell pepper, thinly
  sliced
1 small, sweet onion,
  thinly sliced
a small bunch of
  scallions, sliced
a small bunch of
  cilantro
2 medium garlic
  cloves, minced
2 tbsp soy sauce or
  tamari
2 tbsp rice vinegar
2 tbsp sugar
2 tbsp gochugaru
1 tbsp toasted sesame
  oil
2 tbsp toasted sesame
  seeds
salt and pepper
some toasted seeds
  (page 19), for serving
  (optional)

Preheat the oven to 400°F on the convection setting.

In a bowl, whisk together all the marinade ingredients. Add the cauliflower pieces and toss to coat. Place on a lined baking sheet and roast for about 20 minutes, until cooked and golden brown.

Meanwhile, make the salsa by combining all the ingredients in a bowl, then set to one side.

Make the Korean slaw. Combine the cabbage, carrot, bell pepper, onion, scallions, and cilantro in a large bowl and mix well. Combine the garlic, soy sauce, vinegar, sugar, gochugaru, sesame oil, and sesame seeds in a small bowl and mix. Pour the dressing over the veggies and mix well. Season with salt and black pepper. Scatter toasted seeds over if you like.

Mash the avocados in a small bowl and add the lime juice.

Warm the tortillas for a few minutes in your oven. To serve, lay everything on the table in bowls and build your own tacos. I like to spread the mashed avocado on a tortilla, then load with the roasted cauliflower and a large spoonful of the mango salsa.

Image on pages 88–89 →

Turmeric, ginger + citrus muffins

Turmeric, ginger, and citrus are a powerhouse trio of immunity support. Packed into muffins with a sweet-sharp glaze on top, these tasty snacks will make snack-time treats feel virtuous!

2½ cups all-purpose flour
2½ tsp baking powder
¾ tsp baking soda
½ tsp salt
½ cup plus 1 tbsp vegan butter, melted
scant 1 cup superfine sugar
¾ cup plus 1 tbsp plant-based milk
zest and juice of 3 lemons
zest and juice of 1 large orange
1 tsp ground ginger
1 tsp ground turmeric

Glaze:
1 cup confectioners' sugar
¼ tsp ground turmeric
juice of 1 lemon or orange

Preheat the oven to 350°F on the convection setting and grease a 12-cup muffin tin or line it with paper liners.

Add all the dry ingredients to a bowl and the wet ingredients to another.

Pour the wet mixture into the dry mixture and gently fold together until you can't see any dry flour.

Fill the muffin wells nearly to the top with the batter. Bake for about 18 minutes until the muffins are cooked through and a skewer inserted into the center comes out clean. Remove from the oven and let cool for 10 minutes in the pan before gently transferring to a wire rack. Let cool for 30 minutes.

While the muffins are cooling, make the glaze by adding the confectioners' sugar and turmeric to a small bowl. Add the lemon or orange juice slowly while mixing, making sure you don't have any lumps. Use a teaspoon to drizzle the glaze over the cooled muffins.

MAKE YOUR OWN SAGE STICKS AND RESET THE ENERGY

Burning white sage is a method that has been used for centuries and by many cultures around the world to help clear out negative energy. I love the ritual of cleansing the energy in my home after someone has been unwell, or to create a positive space for a new beginning. It's very powerful and uplifting, and I find it can totally reset the vibe. Burning medicinal herbs also releases antibacterial properties, so there's science behind its healing properties.

Today, burning white sage has become pretty popular, which has unfortunately led to the mass production of sage smudge sticks, often depleting the sacred sources of Native American tribes. Try my sustainable homemade herb bundles instead, and use them to cleanse your home and set new intentions as you progress through your journey to peak wellness. (If you do want to buy a sage stick, make sure you get it from a responsible supplier.)

A few safety guidelines

- Open a window—this acts as good ventilation and lets the old or negative energy flow out.

- The herbs should be gently smoking, not actually on fire.

- As you burn your herbs, hold a flame- and heatproof dish underneath to catch any bits that drop off. When you've finished, fully extinguish the herbs in the dish.

HOMEMADE HERB BUNDLES

You can make a few sticks at a time and store them for later.

Gather together a few sprigs of white sage, about 6 inches long. (I also like to add a few stems of other herbs and plants, such as rosemary, eucalyptus, and lavender—they smell amazing and have other medicinal and cleansing properties.) Tie the stems together with some natural twine or string, and then wrap the twine or string around your herb bundle to hold it all in place. Hang them up upside down somewhere cool and let them dry completely—this will take about two weeks. Then they're ready to use.

To use: Light the leafy end and let it burn a little, then blow out the flame. The herbs should be gently smoking. Starting at your front door—or the door to the room—waft the smoking herbs around the space, making sure to get into every corner to release any trapped energy. (Don't forget behind doors and under desks and tables.) Work your way methodically around the space, ending at an open window.

As you are cleansing the space, you can also choose to say some positive words out loud (or repeat them in your head) to set the new intention for the space. Think about filling the space with positivity, warmth, and love.

Afterward, cleanse yourself and the people in your home in the same way.

CHAPTER 3

Staying Well

Funky ferments 102
  Gut-loving sauerkraut •
  Raving radish pickle •
  Carrot + ginger kimchi •
  Pickled cucumbers

Immunity-boosting
breakfast bars 104

Crunchy root tray bake +
immunity-protection
dressing 107

Barley + miso "risotto"
with greens and crispy
shrooms 112

Chunky turmeric, lentil +
lemon immunity-boost
soup 113

Shiitake mushroom +
seaweed stir-fry 114

Build your own nourish
bowl 121

Shrooms + miso broth
with roasted ginger
squash, sticky crispy
tofu + noodles 124

Healing dhal + banana
chutney 126

Super-nourish chocolate
pudding 129

Staying well

When you're feeling in good health and are well rested, the temptation can be to say yes to everything—social events, work projects, that extra drink on a night out. I know I've been there many times in my life. Packing every minute of the day can take its toll, though, and quickly get you into a cycle of highs and lows, where you roller coaster from energetic phases to having to retreat and recover again while you regroup. Life will always have an element of this—no one's life is a constant all the time, and to live too steadily runs the risk of there never being any excitement or adventure—but there are ways I've learned to maintain a bit more equilibrium and to avoid those dreaded crashes.

This chapter is about establishing solid practices around your mental and physical health, so you can shape your lifestyle in a way that brings you more joy and fulfillment, letting go of things that no longer suit you in order to say yes to more of what does. Paying attention not only to what you put into your body through your diet but also how you can strengthen your resilience and find simple ways to boost your immunity will mean you can take on life's challenges with the confidence that you are more likely to be able to cope with any issues that arise.

We'll look at setting appropriate boundaries and creating a living or work space that inspires your creativity, and I'll share some of the secrets I swear by to keep myself in optimum health.

Balance

If you let things get out of balance for too long, you can start to feel stressed and overwhelmed. Life can somehow feel as though it's controlling you, rather than you being in control of your own path. A little bit of stress in our lives is inevitable—and can actually be good for us—but if it's long-term chronic stress keeping you awake at night or giving you that gnawing feeling in your tummy, it can cause all kinds of health issues. Whenever I start to feel as though I'm doing too much or I get that feeling in my gut that something isn't quite right, I go through the following steps to determine what needs shifting to get me back into balance.

Are you eating and drinking properly?
We know if we've been overindulging in things that don't help us. I'm all for a slice of cake and choosing whatever I want on a menu if I'm celebrating, but we can't eat like that all the time without it having a detrimental effect on how we feel. Too much processed or fried food that is high in sugars, salts, and fats or lacking nutrients, protein, and fiber is going to leave you feeling low in energy and depleted of the vitamins and minerals you need. It will also impact your immune system, leaving you more susceptible to infections. So take an honest look at what you're eating and drinking and get yourself back on track. Try one of the smoothies on pages 62–3 or a power juice from pages 33–4 to kick-start your route back to better nutrition.

Set boundaries
Overstretching ourselves is a short step toward burnout.
Say "no" more often so that you can tune in to what you really need. Setting boundaries on your time and energy is an empowering act and is so important. Don't be afraid to ask for help if you need it either—you'll be surprised how willing people are to help out if they can.

Wave goodbye to toxic people and situations

Are there people or situations in your life that make you feel worse about yourself when you come away from them? Life is too short. Surround yourself with people who lift you up and try to reduce the time you spend in environments that don't serve you any more. However, if there are people or situations in your family or workplace that make you feel uncomfortable, then I know it's not always so simple. If you think having a conversation might help resolve issues, that's a great place to start, but if that's just not possible, know that you can still set some healthy boundaries on your exposure to those situations. Also know that you are ultimately in control of how you respond and react to external environments. Identify ways to regulate your stress levels when you are around those people, and practice ways to de-stress after spending time with them. (See page 46 for the healing power of breathwork.)

Get moving

No surprises here, but exercise—even gentle movement—really does make us feel better, and can protect against illness and make us more resilient to fighting infection. Try some gentle stretches or a quick walk outside and build yourself up from there. See pages 80–1 for more ideas.

Don't ignore a situation

If there's something big that's worrying you, address it. There's no point ignoring it and hoping it goes away, as this will almost always make you feel worse. Talk to the right people, get advice and make a plan so you feel more in control.

What are your core priorities?

There aren't many silver linings to being unwell, but if we are looking for one, then spending so much time inside our own heads can sometimes lead us toward some revelations about what is really important to us. When we're ill, we often can't wait to be well again so that we can do a particular activity or see a certain person again. These are your core priorities. I find journaling really helpful in clarifying what is truly important to me, and then I set mini goals to make sure those things play a bigger part in my life.

THE IMPORTANCE OF GOOD GUT HEALTH

Our gut plays an essential role in our all-body health and well-being. It's now thought that around 70 to 80 percent of our immune cells are found in our gut, and that gut health impacts many vital systems in our body, including our mood. There is lots of evidence linking our gut to our brain, with science behind that "gut feeling" we get when we instinctively know something is right or wrong. It is thought that our gut is responsible for making a lot of our happy hormone, serotonin, too. Creating a thriving, happy, diverse microbiome is one of the very best ways we can support our immunity in the long term, and it may also improve brain function and our mental well-being at the same time. The easiest way to do this is through the food we eat. Aim to include both probiotics (full of live, healthy bacteria) and prebiotics (foods that will feed your existing gut bacteria) in your diet. Here are the top-ten foods I eat to keep my gut bacteria happy.

1. Sea moss and seaweed
Both of these are good sources of fiber and probiotics to feed our existing gut bacteria and replenish the good bacteria. (See page 164 for more on why I love seaweed!)

2. Raw apple cider vinegar
Unpasteurized apple cider vinegar is a source of both prebiotics and probiotics. Don't drink it neat as this can damage your teeth, but dilute with water or juice, or try Gem's immunity-protection dressing on page 19.

3. Sauerkraut, kimchi, and other pickled veg
So easy to make. They go with everything, from sandwiches to tacos to burgers—try my Funky ferments on page 102 for extra fiber and probiotics.

4. Kombucha
A fermented drink made with tea, sugar, bacteria, and yeast, it is full of antioxidants and probiotics to boost gut health, improve immune function, and aid good digestion.

5. Water kefir
Another fizzy fermented drink and an alternative to dairy-based kefir, this is made from water kefir grains. It contains a probiotic called *Lactobacillus casei*, which helps boost immunity and maintains the balance of good bacteria in your gut.

6. Tempeh
Made from fermented soybeans and rich in probiotics and fiber.

7. Miso
A fermented soybean paste, which I use in broths, soups, and delicious whipped miso butter—see pages 28, 41, 112, and 124.

8. Yogurt with active cultures
If you don't eat dairy products, choose dairy-free yogurts that have had live cultures added to help support your gut health.

9. Garlic
A powerful antioxidant, garlic is well known for its immunity-boosting powers, and I use it in lots of my cooking. It is also an amazing prebiotic, keeping your gut bacteria happy—especially if eaten raw. Try it in the Korean slaw on page 87 or Gem's immunity-protection dressing on page 19.

10. Fruits, vegetables, beans and legumes, and whole grains
Basing your diet around high-fiber foods will always keep your gut and digestive system happy. Eat a wide range of colorful fruits and veg to give your gut bacteria the variety of different phytochemicals it needs to flourish. Onions, beans, lentils, and bananas are particularly good for your gut.

FUNKY FERMENTS

Crunchy and vibrantly colorful, these easy ferments are a delicious way to load up on gut-friendly probiotics. Keep a jar in your fridge and add a generous spoonful to sandwiches, salads, grain bowls, noodle dishes, on top of burgers, to glam up your avocado toast, on tacos or nachos . . . the list goes on. You can improve pretty much any meal—as well as your mood, gut health, and digestion—with the addition of these sweet–sour flavor-packed immunity dynamos. (See page 100 for more on the benefits of good gut health.)

EACH RECIPE WILL MAKE 1 LARGE JAR

- You will need a large jar with an airtight top. I use flip-top glass jars.

- Set aside to ferment at room temperature, away from direct sunlight, for the time stated in the recipe.

- When they start to ferment, bubbles will begin to form and it will develop a slightly sour smell. Once you see and smell the signs that your kimchi or pickle is actively fermenting, transfer the jar to the fridge.

- They will keep in the jar for 2 weeks in the fridge.

Gut-loving sauerkraut

—

Prep time: 10 minutes

1 green cabbage
1 tbsp salt
2 tbsp sliced jalapeños

Discard the outer leaves of the
cabbage and slice thinly. Place in a
large bowl. Add the salt and massage
the cabbage for a few minutes. Leave
for a few hours. Mix in the jalapeños
and pack into your jar. Cover and set
aside to ferment for 1 week.

Raving radish pickle

—

Prep time: 10 minutes
Cook time: 1 minute

4 bunches of red radishes, sliced
1 tsp peppercorns
½ tsp mustard seeds
1 cup white vinegar
1 cup water
2½ tbsp cane sugar
1 tbsp salt
1 bay leaf

Put the sliced radishes, peppercorns,
and mustard seeds in a bowl. Heat the
vinegar, water, sugar, and salt in a pan
over medium heat until the sugar and
salt dissolve, about 1 minute. Pour this
brine over the radishes. Add your bay
leaf and let cool. Pour into your jar.
Cover and set aside overnight before
eating.

Carrot + ginger kimchi

—

Prep time: 5 minutes

1 tbsp salt
2 cups water
1 tsp soy sauce or tamari
3 pounds carrots, grated
1-inch piece fresh ginger, grated
2 scallions, thinly sliced
2 garlic cloves, thinly sliced
1 tsp red pepper flakes

In a large bowl, mix all the
ingredients well and then pack into
your jar and pop the lid on. Set aside
to ferment for 48 hours.

Pickled cucumbers

—

Prep time: 5 minutes
Cook time: 1 minute

⅓ cup apple cider vinegar
1 cup water
2 tbsp sugar
2 tsp salt
2 cucumbers, sliced
1 bay leaf

Heat the vinegar, water, sugar,
and salt in a pan over medium heat,
until the sugar and salt dissolve. Put
the cucumbers in a jar. Pour the brine
over the cucumbers. Add your bay
leaf, let cool, and pour into your jar.
Cover and set aside overnight and
they will be ready to eat.

Immunity-boosting breakfast bars

For those days when everything feels like a rush, keep these bars in a jar so you don't miss out on your morning nutrition. Chewy and sweet, dried fruits and oats will release energy slowly, keeping you going until lunch. Goji berries, seeds, and turmeric will give your immune system a boost too. Play around with different seeds and dried fruits (dried apricots or raisins work well) to make them your own. They're great for taking on walks too—keep a few wrapped in your pocket and hand them around when people start to flag!

1½ cups rolled oats
¾ cup nuts (I use walnuts; almonds are also good)
2 tbsp goji berries
12 Medjool dates, pitted and chopped
2 tbsp chia seeds
⅓ cup pumpkin seeds
2½ tbsp hemp seeds
½ tsp ground turmeric
¼ cup maple syrup or honey
1 tbsp unrefined coconut oil
¼ cup nut butter (any)

Preheat the oven 350°F on the convection setting and line an 8-inch square dish with parchment paper.

Toast your oats and nuts on a baking sheet in the oven for 13 to 15 minutes or until slightly golden brown.

Place the oats, nuts, gojis, and dates in a large bowl. Add the seeds and turmeric and set aside.

In a pan, combine the maple syrup, coconut oil, and nut butter and heat over medium heat, stirring constantly, until the mixture begins to bubble. Pour over the oat mixture and mix well.

Put the mixture into the lined dish and press down well. Cover with more parchment paper and then flatten some more. I often place a book on top. Chill in the freezer for 15 minutes to harden and then chop into 12 bars.

Crunchy root tray bake + immunity-protection dressing

An easy, no-fuss, one-pan meal of joyful, colorful root veg, drizzled with my go-to immunity dressing. Great hot or cold, it's perfect for packed lunches too.

---

4 medium carrots, halved lengthwise
1 medium celeriac, peeled and cut into cubes
2 medium white onions, cut into chunks
1 medium beet, peeled and cut into cubes
2 garlic cloves, sliced
2 tbsp olive oil
14-ounce can butter beans, drained and rinsed
leaves from 2 sprigs thyme
salt and pepper
Gem's immunity-protection dressing (page 19), to serve

Preheat the oven to 400°F on the convection setting.

Put all the veggies and the garlic in a large roasting pan. Drizzle with the oil and season with salt and pepper. Roast for 30 to 40 minutes. Then add the butter beans and thyme and roast for another 5 minutes.

To serve, put a heap of the roasted veggies and beans in a bowl and pour the dressing over.

Build

I like to think of the process of healing myself from a period of illness and then rebuilding, maintaining and improving my health and immunity as a series of small steps or building blocks, stacking them one by one until I have a strong immunity defense around me. Supporting your immune system doesn't mean having to suddenly overhaul your entire life all at once, which can feel overwhelming and off-putting—and I seriously doubt you need to do that anyway! Even a few small changes and additions to what you're already doing will reap impressive results. Maybe start with including a few more veggies in your diet, prioritizing rest or establishing healthy boundaries with your time. You can then build on these foundations and gradually introduce more of the activities and practices that you know will make you feel stronger and happier.

One of the most visible ways you can really track your progress is through doing something physical, as you can see your strength and fitness improve over time. Regularly getting active is absolutely vital to good, lasting immunity. Don't overdo it, but don't underestimate your capabilities either. If you push yourself a little bit outside your comfort zone—maybe run that extra five minutes or swim an extra length in the pool—I promise you'll feel amazing afterward. And once you build a little more confidence in your physical capabilities, you'll find that confidence will quickly spread to other areas of your life too. You'll be surprised by what you can achieve!

MEDICINAL MUSHROOMS

Known as the "forgotten superfood," studies have shown that medicinal mushrooms have so many amazing health benefits. Although there is much scientific research still to be done, the knowledge of their superpowers is nothing new: they have been used for more than 5,000 years in Eastern medicine. They are now becoming very popular here too, and almost mainstream in wellness circles. (Just to make it clear, the medicinal mushrooms that I am talking about are not the ones that make you hallucinate and are 100 percent legal to use!)

If you've been following me on Instagram for a while, you'll know how much I love mushrooms. I talk about them all the time! I've been using them for about five years to turbo-boost my immune system and overall health, and have seen amazing improvements in my energy, sleep, skin, and immune strength.

There's a huge variety out there online, with lots of misinformation and radical claims being made. To make things simple, I've listed my top six medicinal mushrooms to improve your health and boost immunity.

How to use: I buy my mushrooms in powder form or as a tincture. Different mushrooms have different potencies, so always read the packet for how much to use. I usually add them to smoothies or teas, use them in energy balls, or add to broths and stews.

Reishi
Probably the best all-around medicinal mushroom, reishi has been used for thousands of years to support the immune system, reduce stress, and promote calm. It is thought to be so powerful that it is known as the "mushroom of immortality"!

Chaga
Believed to be the highest natural source of antioxidants, I swear chaga has increased my energy levels since I've been taking it. It's also great

for skin health and protects against the aging process. It helps reduce inflammation and is the king of boosting the immune system.

Lion's mane
If you find yourself losing focus during the day or your mind is a bit foggy, try lion's mane to enhance your mental abilities, support cognitive function, and improve your mood.

Turkey tail
Another brilliant all-arounder for healing, supporting the immune system, and gut health. One of the most researched mushrooms, turkey tail has even been used in some studies of cancer patients, alongside conventional treatment, with impressive results due to its immunity-boosting powers.

Tremella
Full of antioxidants and rich in vitamin D, this mushroom supports healthy glowing skin and helps restore energy levels. It is also thought to promote good lung, stomach, and kidney function.

Cordyceps
A very potent mushroom that, according to traditional medicine, will awaken your core energy, boost physical strength and performance, and even increase your sex drive.

Everyday mushrooms

The mushrooms that we use in cooking all the time, such as button, chestnut, and portobello, are a great source of nutrients. They are high in vitamin D, great for gut health and rich in B vitamins. They also contain the mineral selenium, which helps support the immune system and boosts your mood. The following mushrooms are actually considered medicinal mushrooms, but you can buy them in most supermarkets:

Shiitake mushrooms
These powerful mushrooms will help protect against cell damage and boost the immune system, and they are rich in B vitamins.

Oyster mushrooms
Used in traditional medicine to treat high cholesterol and diabetes and to fight infections, they are a great all-around immunity booster.

Tip: Grow-your-own-mushroom kits have become very popular and there are so many available online. It's a really fun introduction to growing mushrooms and the results are incredible. They're also a great gift if you have any mushroom-loving friends.

What to look for when buying mushroom supplements

- **Beta-D-glucans.** Make sure to buy medicinal-mushroom products that are active. Look for their beta-D-glucans count rather than polysaccharides.

- **Strong color and taste.** Intense color and flavor are signs of potency.

- **Fruiting body only.** The fruiting body contains the highest level of beneficial compounds.

- **Natural habitat and organically grown.** Mushrooms absorb minerals from wherever they are grown. Organic, wood-grown mushrooms are believed to result in higher levels of active compounds.

Note: Although medicinal mushrooms are generally considered safe to take when pregnant, there is limited research available. Speak to your doctor before taking any supplements if you are pregnant or breastfeeding, if you have any other health conditions, or if you are taking medication.

Barley + miso "risotto" with greens and crispy shrooms

Pearl barley makes such a great twist on a classic risotto, providing iron and B vitamins to boost your energy levels and your mood. The white miso will give your gut some TLC and peas are a great source of zinc. Our bodies don't store excess zinc, so it's important to include it regularly in our diets to support our immune systems.

2 tbsp olive oil
4 garlic cloves, minced
½-inch piece fresh ginger, peeled and grated
7 ounces scallions, thinly sliced
1 tsp mixed dried herbs
¾ cup pearl barley
2½ cups veggie stock
2 tbsp miso paste (I use white)
2 tbsp nutritional yeast
5 ounces frozen peas
1¾ ounces mushrooms, sliced (I like shiitake, but any will do)
salt and pepper
chopped fresh parsley, to serve

Heat 1 tablespoon of the olive oil in a pot over medium heat and add the garlic, ginger, and scallions, along with a pinch of salt and the dried herbs. Sauté for 5 minutes. Add the barley and half the stock. Bring to a low boil and cook for 10 minutes, then pour in the rest of the stock.

Reduce the heat, cover with a lid, and cook for 20 minutes until the barley is nice and soft. If you need to add more liquid, add a little water.

Stir the miso and nutritional yeast together to mix (you may need to whisk the miso until dissolved). Add this to the pot, along with the peas. Cook for a few minutes while you make the crispy shrooms.

Heat the remaining 1 tablespoon oil in a skillet. Add the mushrooms and season with salt and pepper. Cook over high heat for a few minutes either side until they are a little crispy and golden brown.

To serve, spoon the risotto into a bowl and add the crispy shrooms and fresh parsley on top, with a little pepper.

Chunky turmeric, lentil + lemon immunity-boost soup

Every spoonful of this nourishing, revitalizing soup is brimming with antioxidants to supercharge your immune system. Comforting and cozy from the spices, sweet potato, and lentils, but with a zing from the lemon, it'll give you strength and make you feel alive!

2 tbsp olive oil
1 onion, finely diced
3 garlic cloves, minced
2 carrots, chopped
3 celery stalks, sliced
7 ounces sweet
  potatoes, peeled and
  finely diced
2 tsp ground cumin
1 tsp ground turmeric
1-inch piece fresh
  ginger, peeled and
  grated
4 cups veggie stock
¾ cup dried red lentils
14-ounce can tomatoes
1 tbsp tomato puree
5 ounces kale, chopped
3½ ounces baby
  spinach
a handful of fresh
  parsley
juice of 1 lemon
salt and pepper

Heat the olive oil in a large pan over medium heat and add the onion, garlic, carrots, celery, sweet potatoes, and spices. Sauté for 5 minutes, stirring frequently.

Add the stock and lentils, canned tomatoes, and tomato puree. Stir well and bring to a boil.

Turn the heat to low, put the lid on, and simmer for about 15 minutes. The lentils and sweet potatoes should be soft and cooked, but not mushy. Add the kale, spinach, parsley, and lemon juice. Season with a pinch each of salt and pepper to taste and cook for a further 5 minutes before serving.

Shiitake mushroom + seaweed stir-fry

This is one of my all-time-favorite super-speedy suppers. Even though it's incredibly quick to make, it's absolutely packed full of rich umami flavors and complex nutrition to give you the ultimate turbo-boost of goodness. Shiitake mushrooms are medicinal mushrooms that in Chinese medicine are believed to help you live longer (see page 109 for more on why I'm obsessed with mushrooms!). Seaweed provides so many vital nutrients that are often missing from our diets, and they also add a delicious salty tang (see page 164 for more on seaweed's superfood status).

1 tbsp toasted sesame oil

12 ounces shiitake mushrooms (or 5 ounces dried, soaked in warm water for 20 minutes, then drained)

4 scallions

1-inch piece fresh ginger, peeled and finely chopped

3½ ounces kale, finely sliced

1 tbsp soy sauce or tamari

10½ ounces cooked noodles (any kind; I like udon)

2 tbsp seaweed flakes

sesame seeds, to serve

In a wok or large skillet, heat the sesame oil over medium-high heat and then add the mushrooms, scallions, ginger, and kale. Cook until softened, then add the tamari and cooked noodles and stir until the noodles are coated.

Stir in the seaweed and serve immediately. Season with extra soy sauce and sesame seeds.

This tastes just as delicious if you substitute the noodles for cooked brown rice.

Invigorate

If you've been following the tips and strategies in this book so far, you should hopefully be starting to feel and see some of the benefits of increased energy and focus, better digestion, more restful sleep, and generally feeling less stressed out in the face of modern life. You may even be feeling up for taking on more exciting challenges, trying something new, and expanding your experiences!

When I'm feeling upbeat and energized, or before I start a new project, I like to make sure my living area and workspace reflect where I am right now and continue to inspire me. That could mean creating a more relaxing, calming space in my bedroom so that I can get the rest I need during a busy patch, or finding ways to encourage creativity where I work. If you look around your home and it stresses you out, then that's not going to help support your ongoing wellness.

Get organized

I love a tidy workspace near a window for some natural daylight. I open up the windows to let in fresh air every day, and before a new project I cleanse my work space with a sage stick (see page 92). If you have the space, moving a few bits of furniture around can give you a whole new outlook.

Live the rainbow

The colors you choose to have in your home can have an enormous impact on how you feel. Blues, greens, and calming pinks are harmonious and balancing, whereas reds, oranges, and yellows are stimulating and creative. White is thought to give us more clarity. You can change the whole feel and energy of your space very quickly by painting the walls—but if that sounds too much of an investment, you could just add some pops of color with cushions, some new bedding, or a picture for the wall.

Minimalist or maximalist?
Do you like to have clean, almost empty surfaces, or to fill your home with memories and objects you have collected? There's absolutely nothing wrong with either, but if you're living in a space that goes against your natural preferences, then that could be impacting how you feel on a daily basis. Also, just because you like to have lots of your things around you doesn't mean it has to be messy! A chaotic room can make my mind feel messy too, and even a quick ten-minute tidy-up of my desk area can make me feel less overwhelmed. But remember that if your house is full of people, each living their own lives, it's almost impossible for it to be tidy all the time!

What makes you happy?
Looking around my living room always makes me happy. I can see our music collection, our "Be Grateful" neon sign, things we've brought back from holidays, the kids' pictures, and photos of friends and family. Surrounding myself with the things that make me happy reminds me of the good times, even when things feel tough.

Plants, plants, and more plants!
They make me feel so happy and it's been scientifically proven that plants are good for us. They increase the oxygen in our homes and help eliminate toxins. Looking at greenery is good for our brains, and caring for a plant can even improve our mental well-being. Double points if you grow something you can also eat, like herbs, salad veg, or even mushrooms—we grow shiitake and oyster mushrooms at home using a kit!

TOP FIVE EASY PLANTS
TO KEEP ALIVE

1. **Spider plant.** Produces lots of spider babies that you can give away as gifts and has impressive air-purifying abilities.

2. **Snake plant.** Cleans the air and has the unique ability to release oxygen at night, so it's a good one for the bedroom. (Be aware that its leaves are poisonous to children and pets.)

3. **Aloe vera.** Purifies the air and you can use the gel on burns or to soothe mild skin complaints. Or add it to smoothies—it contains calcium, magnesium, selenium, and zinc, among other minerals.

4. **Monstera.** Also known as a Swiss cheese plant. For something larger, with impact, I love its big glossy leaves. (Be aware that its leaves are poisonous to children and pets.)

5. **Cacti and succulents.** Available in a huge range of shapes and sizes, they are almost impossible to kill—you can forget to water these and they won't mind. (Obviously keep spiky plants away from children and pets.)

Natural cleaning products

We've all been a bit obsessed with keeping our hands and homes clean in recent years because of the pandemic. Bottles of antibacterial hand sanitizer in our bags have become the norm and intensive cleaning sprays line the shelves of our homes. If you're looking for something a bit less chemical, try these natural alternatives.

Antibacterial all-purpose cleaner
—
Mix together 3 cups of water and ½ cup white vinegar in a glass spray bottle. Add 10 to 15 drops of tea tree, clove, or lavender essential oil. Shake to combine. Spray onto surfaces and wipe away with a damp cloth. Change it up by adding lemon or wild orange aromatherapy oil instead of lavender for a fresh, uplifting citrus smell.

For bathrooms, kitchens, and unclogging sinks
—
Mix ½ cup baking soda with 1 cup white vinegar. Use right away as the two will fizz together. You can also make a paste, using less vinegar, and apply to more stubborn areas. Use a cloth or sponge to wipe away and rinse with warm water.

Handwash
—
Mix ½ cup castile soap with 1½ tablespoons almond oil and 15 drops each of tea tree oil, clove oil, and peppermint oil in a soap dispenser and give it a really good shake. You can also make this with other essential oils—I like lavender or orange.

BUILD YOUR OWN NOURISH BOWL

These healing bowls are a staple of my Nourish Package and a regular in our house. Changing through the seasons, building your own nourish bowl means you can mix-and-match whatever ingredients you feel your body is calling out for today. Below is some guidance and ideas, but what I love about nourish bowls is that they let you be creative—the more colorful they are, the more appetizing they will look and taste. Choose seasonal veggies and whatever you have in your fridge, and don't be afraid to experiment.

For a healthy balance of flavors and nutrition, choose at least one item from each list on pages 122–123 to provide you with good fats, proteins, grains, and veggies. I often batch-prep a few key ingredients (such as the butter beans, roasted sweet potatoes or squash, and chopped salad) and keep them in the fridge to make up lunch bowls like this during the week. Ingredients can be served warm or cold depending on the season and what your body is craving.

Protein: 2 tbsp per bowl
—
- 14-ounce can chickpeas roasted with 1 tsp olive oil, 1 tsp smoked paprika, and 1 chopped garlic clove

- Healing dhal (page 126)

- Easy hummus (page 15)

- Crispy tofu (page 125)

- 14-ounce can butter beans cooked with 14-ounce can tomatoes, ½ tsp chili powder, 2 chopped garlic cloves, drizzle of olive oil, squeeze of fresh lemon juice, and a handful of chopped fresh parsley

Grains: 2 tbsp per bowl
—
- Steamed quinoa mixed with chopped fresh parsley, fresh lemon juice, and a drizzle of olive oil

- Cooked brown rice fried with ½ onion, 2 garlic cloves, coconut oil, ½ tsp ground cinnamon, ½ tsp ground cumin, and ½ tsp ground turmeric

- Whole wheat pasta tossed with olive oil and salt or pesto

- Noodles tossed with toasted sesame oil and soy sauce

- Pearl barley (leftover "risotto," page 112, would work well)

- Bulgur wheat

Healthy fats: 1 tbsp per bowl
—
- 1 avocado, halved

- Tzatziki: 1 tbsp coconut yogurt, 1 tbsp olive oil, juice of 1 lemon, chopped fresh parsley and dill, ½ cucumber, cubed

- 1 tbsp almond butter

- 1 tbsp mixed nuts

- Tahini, on its own or whisked with a little maple syrup or coconut yogurt

Veggies
—
Make these seasonal with what you have in your crisper.

- Sweet potatoes, halved and roasted with a drizzle of olive oil, 1 tbsp honey, and garlic cloves

- Butternut squash or pumpkin, peeled and roasted with a drizzle of olive oil, 1 tsp ground cinnamon, and salt

- Carrots roasted with their skin on and seasoned with za'atar

- Crunchy root tray bake (page 107)

- Chopped salad: cucumber, ripe tomatoes, and lots of chopped fresh parsley, mixed with olive oil, salt, and lemon zest and juice, then add to dhal

- Roasted cauliflower (pages 86–87)

Greens

—

- Use whatever is in season, e.g., kale, spinach, chard, or cavolo nero, sautéed in olive oil, garlic, and a little ginger, finished with fresh lemon juice

- Steamed or roasted broccoli, tossed with toasted sesame oil and sesame seeds

- Steamed green beans, dressed with olive oil, lemon juice, and salt

- Grilled or pan-fried zucchini

- Simple spinach side (page 76)

Extras

—

- Gem's immunity-protection dressing (page 19)

- Immunity-boosting green goddess dressing (page 18)

- Toasted nuts or seeds (page 19)

- Drizzle of Nut butter (page 18) or tahini

- Funky ferments (pages 102–3)

- Chopped fresh herbs

- Plantain chips—sliced plantain browned in coconut oil and a little ground cinnamon (these make a great snack too!)

Shrooms + miso broth with roasted ginger squash, sticky crispy tofu + noodles

Give your system a full-body wake-up with this intensely flavored noodle broth. Miso, seaweed, mushrooms, ginger, garlic, and chile will get you fired up and ready to take on anything! Cooking everything in the broth means you don't lose any valuable nutrients either—and there's so much goodness going on here. I've given two options for toppings: roasted squash and sticky tofu. You can serve it with either, both, or neither, depending on how hungry you are. If you're going to serve it with only the tofu, double the recipe to make enough for four people.

4 cups veggie broth
3 tbsp miso paste
1 piece of seaweed
(e.g., kombu)
3½ ounces mushrooms,
thinly sliced (I like
shiitake)
1¾ ounces noodles
(I like udon)
3½ ounces kale, sliced

Squash topping:
1 small squash
1 tbsp olive oil
3 garlic cloves, sliced
2-inch piece fresh
ginger, peeled and
grated

Sticky crispy tofu:
1 block firm tofu, cut
into 1-inch cubes
2 tbsp tamari or soy
sauce
3 tbsp cornstarch
1 garlic clove, finely
chopped, or 1 tsp
garlic powder
2 tbsp olive oil
1 tbsp sesame seeds

Garnish:
1 red chile, sliced
1 scallion, sliced

If you're making the squash topping, preheat the oven to 400°F on the convection setting. Cut the squash in half and use a spoon to scoop out the seeds. Cut the skin off the squash with a peeler or small knife. Cut the squash into thick slices. In a bowl, mix the squash with the olive oil, garlic, and 1 tablespoon of the ginger. Line a baking sheet with parchment paper and spread the squash over the parchment. Roast for about 20 minutes until cooked and golden brown. Remove from the oven and set aside.

In a large pan, add the veggie broth, miso paste, and seaweed and whisk until the paste is dissolved completely. Add the sliced mushrooms, the remaining ginger, and the noodles to the broth, cover, and simmer over low heat for 5 minutes or until the noodles are cooked. Remove from the heat and add the kale.

If you want to make the sticky crispy tofu, put the tofu cubes and tamari in a small bowl. In another medium bowl, add the cornstarch and garlic, stir well, and set aside.

Place a large nonstick skillet over medium heat. Add the olive oil. Add the tofu cubes to the cornstarch mixture and gently stir to coat, then transfer to the skillet and cook until browned, to 3 minutes. Turn over and cook until browned on the other side, 2 to 3 minutes more. Sprinkle the sesame seeds over the cooked tofu.

Top the broth with a few slices of the roasted squash and/or sticky tofu and garnish with the red chile and scallion.

SERVES 4 | *Prep time: 30 minutes* | *Cook time: 30 minutes*

Healing dhal + banana chutney

When you need to spend some time looking inward, this restorative dhal will help create the reflective headspace you need. The spices and lentils will supercharge your immune system, and being high in folate and iron means they will energize you and give you strength. The banana chutney is heavenly—my mom used to serve chopped banana with curry and I've been a convert ever since!

1 tbsp olive oil
2 onions, finely
  chopped
1-inch piece ginger,
  peeled and minced
1 celery stalk, finely
  chopped
1½ cups dried red
  lentils
2 tbsp curry powder
1 tbsp ground turmeric
1 tbsp garam masala
3 cups veggie stock
13½-ounce can
  coconut milk

Banana chutney:
fresh cilantro
½ red onion, chopped
  small
1 red chile, chopped
1 large banana,
  chopped
juice of 1 lime

Heat the oil in a pan over medium heat. Add the onions, ginger, and celery.

Cook until the onions are soft, then add the lentils and spices and stir so that the lentils don't get stuck to the bottom of the pan.

Start adding the veggie stock little by little and stirring constantly. The dhal will start to get thicker and the lentils will soften. Stir in the coconut milk and cook for 15 to 20 minutes. Add some water if it gets too thick.

To make the banana chutney, mix all the ingredients in a bowl and add a spoonful to the dhal before serving.

127

Super-nourish chocolate pudding

Sometimes boosting wellness and immunity is as simple as doing things that make you feel good. And these chocolate pots are pure bliss. Cacao has been proven to contain the "bliss chemical," serotonin, and it can boost your immunity, too. Decadent and rich, these are the perfect luxury indulgence.

2½ cups coconut milk
3 tbsp cacao powder
2 tbsp maple syrup
¾ cup chia seeds

Optional toppings:
grated zest of 1 orange
chopped cherries
berries
grated chocolate

In a bowl, whisk together the coconut milk, cacao powder, and maple syrup and then stir in the chia seeds. I use a handheld mixer, but a hand whisk is fine.

Pour into 4 glasses and chill in the fridge for at least 3 hours, until they have firmed up.

Add your desired toppings and serve.

CHAPTER 4

Supercharge

Daily booster shots 138
  Turmeric + ginger • Honey, garlic + lemon • Apple cider vinegar + maple syrup • Pineapple cider vinegar

Superfood pancakes with blueberry compote + coconut whip 140

Super-nourish stir-fry with kimchi 142

Lemon + honey drizzle cake 145

Breakfast banoffee pie jars 150

Sweet potato pasta bake 153

Gem's eggplant parmigiana 154

Super-boost rainbow curry + Brazil nuts + sweet ginger chutney 158

High-vibe cleansing bowl + fermented pickles 160

Cherry Bakewell slice + nice cream 162

Seaweed and sea moss 164
  Seaweed, kimchi + sriracha popcorn • Super seaweed salad dressing • Toasted seaweed chips • Seaweed butter

Supercharge

Get ready to take your immunity and well-being to the next level. These are the magical ingredients and nutrition tips that will give you superpowers and optimize your health. Building on the good foundations you've already established, you can now take those extra steps to feel your best self ever, creating a strong immune system, with even more energy and better mental resilience, so that you can unleash your full potential.

In my nutrition work, I always focus on preventative strategies and am obsessed with learning more about how the foods we eat can give us that extra edge when it comes to how we feel. The ideas and recipes in this chapter are those I've included in my regular routines for a while now. They have given me the energy and enthusiasm to meet daily challenges and encourage me to reach for the life I want. I really hope you find the same!

As always, though, remember that no one can live at full pace 24/7. Revisit earlier sections of this book to make sure you're continuing to cover the basics of good nutrition and self-care, and take time out to rest and recharge properly whenever you need it.

Finding your power

Looking back, it is now obvious to me that I was destined to work with food somehow. Even when I was working as a drug counselor and with sex workers, I always found myself drawn to food. I loved how preparing and sharing meals together encouraged people to feel more comfortable opening up about their often very difficult experiences. And through my own struggles with fertility, the more I learned about food, the more I became fascinated with the potential it has to impact our entire well-being. I now love my job so much—it's what gives me my fire and makes me excited to start each and every day!

What is it that gives you that extra zing and fuel for life? When we're working with our true purpose, everything else seems to fall into place a bit more easily somehow, and it can make our worries feel a little less overwhelming. I know it can seem like a BIG question, but start by finding ways to bring more of what excites you and gets your creativity flowing into your daily life. Doing more of what you enjoy will reduce your stress levels and make you feel happier. It will give you a new focus in life, away from your usual routine— and who knows? It may just be the start of a new career too!

FIVE QUESTIONS
TO HELP YOU FIND
YOUR FIRE

1. If you had more time, what would you want to do more of?

2. If you were talking to your younger self, is there anything that they would be surprised you're not doing now?

3. What achievement are you most proud of in your life?

4. What are three skills or traits that you have that make you different from other people?

5. What is something you'd regret never experiencing?

TEN WAYS TO FIND YOUR PASSION AND EXPERIENCE MORE JOY

Everyday life can sometimes feel relentless, but even if things are difficult right now, introducing a bit of joy can help lighten the load a little, take your mind off things and help keep things in perspective. Not focusing on your worries, even for a short time, can also sometimes lead to some interesting insights and new angles on problems. Try one of these ideas to take yourself out of your head, experience something new and maybe gain some clarity on what might be next for you.

1. What's new?!
Try something that you have always wanted to do but never got around to or have always felt a bit nervous about, like skateboarding or swimming in the ocean. It's never too late and you are never too old! Taking yourself out of your comfort zone really opens up your mind to a whole world of new possibilities (also see pages 146–7 to read more about the benefits of taking a risk).

2. Write a bucket list
Write down 25 things you want to do before a certain time and commit to it.

3. Keep learning
Whether it's going to college or just reading about a new topic online, keep your mind inquisitive—you never know where it might take you.

4. Get creative
Visit an art gallery, have a go at painting, wreath making (it doesn't have to be just at Christmas!), DJ-ing, or flower arranging, or listen to some new music. Whatever you're drawn to, create time to flex that creative muscle. It will enhance your life—and remember, it's about enjoying something, not necessarily being good at it!

5. Feed your spirituality

Whether you follow a particular religion or not, giving yourself over to a higher power can have so many benefits. Maybe start by practicing yoga, going on a retreat, or meditating. It will make you feel so good and can give you time to reflect.

6. Vision boards

I think these are an amazing way to get creative and visualize what you want in the future. I regularly make these to help me focus on where I want to be. Find pictures and phrases that represent your goals, stick them to a piece of paper, and put it somewhere you'll see it often. It'll help keep you focused on your intentions and can really help clarify your direction and decision-making.

7. Write cards and letters

I recently started sending cards and letters to friends. It's such a lovely old-school thing to do and brings me so much joy. It's also a great way to reflect on what I'm doing.

8. Journal

I've written in a journal on and off for years. I find writing down my thoughts really therapeutic, and it helps me find perspective when I'm going through a difficult patch. I also like looking back though what I've written in old journals to find recurring ideas and thoughts, and I use these to shape new plans.

9. Play more games

Games aren't just for kids! Being silly and taking yourself out of your own head for a while is an amazing mood-booster and also a great way to bond with others.

10. Forage at thrift shops and garage sales

I love a bargain and am always on the lookout for pre-loved and vintage clothes, which I sometimes try to customize. I am no fashion designer, but I wear it with happiness!

Bonus tip: Be grateful. I talk about this a lot, but being grateful for what we have is so important. It also helps clarify what those important things are in our life, so we can nurture them and make more time for them.

DAILY BOOSTER SHOTS

Power up with one of my immunity juice shots! Providing an intense dose of vitamins and nutrients, I have one most mornings. They are a delicious way of adding extra immunity support to your diet.

EACH MAKES 4 SHOTS

Store them in fridge for up to 5 days.
Separation is normal: just shake before serving.

Turmeric + ginger
—

Fight off the first signs of a cold. Anti-inflammatory and digestive support. Also good for nausea.

Prep time: 5 minutes

1-inch piece fresh ginger
1½-inch piece fresh turmeric, or 2 tsp ground
juice of 3 lemons
juice of 2 oranges
a pinch of black pepper

Grate the ginger and turmeric. Mix with the remaining ingredients in a glass bottle. Leave in the fridge overnight and then strain through a sieve. Store in a clean bottle. Drink hot or cold, daily.

Honey, garlic + lemon
—

Antibacterial to help you through flu season. Good for coughs and sore throats.

Prep time: 5 minutes

juice of 3 lemons
3 garlic cloves, chopped
½ tsp cayenne pepper
2 tbsp honey (manuka, if you have it)

In a bowl, mix the lemon juice, garlic, and cayenne. Add the honey and stir all the ingredients together well, using a small whisk if you need to. Strain through a sieve and pour into a small bottle.

Apple cider vinegar + maple syrup
—

To give your gut some much needed TLC. Helps regulate blood glucose levels. High in antioxidants and good for general immunity support.

Prep time: 2 minutes

7 tbsp warm water
3 tbsp maple syrup
5 tbsp apple cider vinegar
  (with the mother)
a pinch of ground cinnamon

Add the warm water, maple syrup, vinegar, and cinnamon to a jar. Pop on the lid and shake until the syrup dissolves.

Pineapple cider vinegar
—

High in antioxidants and aids digestion. This is a real immunity boost and will supercharge your system.

Prep time: 2 minutes

7 tablespoons pineapple juice
5 tbsp apple cider vinegar
  (with the mother)
2 tbsp honey
juice of 1 lime
¼ tsp ground turmeric

Put all the ingredients in a large jar, pop on the lid, and shake until well mixed.

Superfood pancakes with blueberry compote + coconut whip

These pancakes are a treat for the eyes as well as the belly! They look like a very fancy brunch, but they're really easy to make. The blueberry compote not only tastes amazing but provides a delicious shot of antioxidants. Perfect for a lazy weekend breakfast—or even as dessert!

scant 1½ cups all-purpose flour
1 tbsp baking powder
½ tsp salt
3 tbsp chia seeds
3 tbsp maple syrup
1½ cups plant-based milk
1 tsp apple cider vinegar
1 tsp vanilla extract
oil, for frying
a handful of seeds (optional)

Blueberry compote:
2 cups frozen blueberries
3½ tbsp water
¼ cup granulated sugar
juice of 1 lemon

Coconut whip:
1 cup coconut yogurt
3½ tbsp plant-based whipping cream
2 tbsp maple syrup, plus extra for drizzling
½ tsp vanilla extract

First make the compote by adding half of the blueberries, water, sugar, and lemon juice to a small pan. Cook over medium heat for about 10 minutes. Add the rest of the blueberries and cook for 5 minutes more, stirring often. Remove from the heat and set aside.

To make the coconut whip, add all the ingredients to a bowl and, using a handheld mixer, beat on high for 4 minutes until the mixture holds soft peaks. Keep in the fridge.

For the pancakes, mix the dry ingredients and the wet ingredients in two separate bowls. Then add the wet mix to the dry and mix well. I use a whisk for this. Let the mixture rest for 10 minutes. Heat a nonstick pan (a pancake pan if you have one) over medium heat. Add a little oil and, once the pan is hot, scoop ¼-cup portions of the batter into the pan.

Cook each pancake until golden brown, about 4 minutes. Flip them and cook for another minute until cooked through and browned on both sides.

To serve, stack the pancakes on top of one another and add a dollop of compote and then coconut whip. Add a drizzle of maple syrup for extra sweetness and a scattering of mixed seeds for some crunch.

Super-nourish stir-fry with kimchi

Good gut health is one of the best ways to help support your all-around well-being. There are so many studies connecting a diverse gut microbiome with strong immunity—and even our mental health (see page 100 for more on this). Spicy and gorgeously green, this quick stir-fry has a real zing and kimchi is an amazing source of probiotics to give your gut the love it deserves. Cashews add crunch and also contain antioxidants.

1 tbsp toasted sesame oil
1 onion, sliced
2 garlic cloves, chopped
9 ounces mushrooms, sliced (I like shiitake)
2 heads bok choy, leaves separated
1 bunch kale, leaves shredded
1 tbsp tamari
2 tbsp cashews
1 tbsp seaweed flakes (dulse)
3 tbsp kimchi
cooked rice, to serve (optional)

Heat the oil in a large skillet or wok over medium-high heat.

Add the onion, garlic, and mushrooms and sauté for 5 minutes.

Reduce the heat to medium and add the bok choy and kale. Sauté for 2 to 3 minutes until the kale wilts.

Add the tamari, cashews, seaweed, and kimchi and stir for 1 to 2 minutes until everything is warm. Serve with rice or on its own.

Lemon + honey drizzle cake

A little honey gives the classic lemon drizzle a tasty twist to one of my all-time favorite cakes—as well as upping its immunity-boosting powers. Really, though, this cake is best eaten with a cup of tea and a do-not-disturb sign for pure indulgence and a moment of time out. You can also eat it warm, without the icing, served with pudding as a dessert.

1⅔ cups all-purpose flour (use gluten-free if you like)
¾ cup almond flour
2 tsp baking soda
a pinch of salt
½ tsp baking powder
½ cup plus 1½ tbsp soft brown sugar
7 tbsp plant-based milk of choice
¾ cup plus 1 tbsp plain yogurt (such as coconut yogurt)
¼ cup unrefined coconut oil, melted
zest and juice of 3 lemons
1 tsp pure vanilla extract

For the drizzle icing:
1 tbsp honey
2 tbsp confectioners' sugar
zest and juice of 2 lemons

Preheat the oven to 340°F on the convection setting and grease a 9-inch loaf pan.

Mix all the dry ingredients in a large bowl. Whisk the liquid ingredients in a separate bowl, and then add the wet to the dry and stir to combine. Pour the batter into the prepared pan and bake for about 50 minutes, until the cake has risen and a toothpick or knife inserted into the middle of the cake comes out clean.

For the icing, mix together all the ingredients in a pan and warm over low heat. Let cool for a few minutes, then pierce a few holes in the top of the still-warm cake and drizzle over the icing, reserving some for later.

Once the cake has cooled, using a teaspoon, drizzle some more icing all over the top, allowing some to drip down the sides.

Courage is letting go of the familiar

Over the past few years, we've all had to learn to live with a lot of uncertainty and it's definitely not been easy for anyone. It's completely natural to find living with constantly shifting horizons a challenge— it's human nature to crave stability and comfort. But I've learned that making yourself take a few big bold steps every now and then and trying to get more comfortable with the idea that life will often throw unexpected plans in your path can leave you more resilient and open to experiences you never thought possible.

When our kids were little, we decided to move to Barcelona for six months— and ended up staying for three years. We had the time of our lives out there and it also started a whole new career for me! I began cooking plant-based picnics for DJs who traveled a lot but were sick of airplane food, and then I did catering for local offices and even set up a mini takeout business from our apartment— and it all snowballed from there for us. When we came back to the UK, I set up Gem's Wholesome Kitchen and here we are seven years later! Without taking that risk to live abroad at that time in our lives, I wonder if I'd have ended up on a different path?

Although I'm now much more comfortable with life being a bit unpredictable and am happier to lean into it and roll with those changes, I've found ways to help anchor myself and feel a bit more secure. Spending time with my family, listening to music, cooking and eating healthy food, getting plenty of fresh air and enough rest, and journaling are the simple ways I have found I can stay grounded. Find what yours are and draw on them during phases of change and uncertainty.

You definitely don't need to suddenly decide to live abroad or quit your job or anything like that, but stepping outside your comfort zone is absolutely something I'd recommend trying regularly. Think about reframing feelings of apprehension as excitement. Do things differently, take more risks (safely of course!), be open to new experiences, and invite a bit more spontaneity and energy into your day. You'll broaden your own horizons and start to see new opportunities where you didn't before, and in turn you'll find that you become a bit more comfortable and able to ride out the storm when things don't go the way you were expecting—as life has a habit of doing!

TAKE A COLD SHOWER

I do this often and it's a great way of getting comfortable with being uncomfortable! You'll feel amazing afterward too. Cold-water therapy releases endorphins, boosts your immunity, improves circulation, and can help you sleep better. It also stimulates the vagus nerve, which activates the parasympathetic system (see page 46 for more on why this is important for immunity and healing). Try it for 30 days, keeping a diary of how you feel, and see the difference at the end.

· Shower as usual and when you're finished, turn the water to cold. Breathe deeply and evenly, focusing on staying calm and clearing your mind. Start by putting in one arm, then the other, then one leg and then step in and spin your body around so you're fully covered.

· Begin with just 10 to 15 seconds and build yourself up a little bit each day. Singing can really help you breathe properly and not get overwhelmed by the cold! I like to finish with a warm shower for a minute or so.

· When you get out of the shower, check in with how you are feeling. Your endorphins should be buzzing!

Maybe you are ready to look into cold-water swimming now?!

IMMUNITY-BOOSTING ADAPTOGENS

Adaptogens are an amazing group of roots, herbs, and mushrooms that can help us respond better to stress and anxiety, feel calmer, boost our energy levels, and support our overall well-being and immunity. They can do all these different things because they are able to "adapt" to whatever your body needs.

Adaptogens tend to grow in difficult environments, learning to react to their individual circumstances and adjust accordingly. Maybe we can learn something from that?! They have been used in Chinese and Ayurvedic medicine for thousands of years and since introducing them into my diet, I've seen so many benefits and feel so much more in balance. I also make sure to take them in the autumn, at the start of cold and flu season, to help prevent illnesses.

I've included a list of my favorites here, but also see the section on plant powders on page 170 to read about maca, nettle powder, and moringa, which are all incredible adaptogens too—as well as the section on medicinal mushrooms on page 109. Available as a powder or tincture, or in their natural state, they can all be added to smoothies, drinks, or raw snacks or used in cooking. Read the package for their individual dosage recommendations, as potency can vary.

Ashwagandha
An evergreen shrub grown in India and Southeast Asia, this is one of the most powerful ancient herbs we know about and is frequently used in traditional medicine. It contains amino acids, herbs, and vitamins that can help the body manage stress, increase our energy levels, improve concentration, lower cholesterol, reduce inflammation, balance blood sugar, and support immunity.

Ginseng
Brimming with antioxidants, ginseng has been used in Chinese medicine for centuries. There are lots of varieties available, the most popular being American ginseng and Asian ginseng, which differ in potency and effect on the body. American ginseng works more as a cooling, calming, relaxing agent, whereas Asian ginseng is invigorating and stimulating. Both types boost

immunity, have an antiaging effect, support heart health, can lower cholesterol, regulate blood sugar levels, support fertility, improve focus and concentration, and help boost your mental health. Wow!

Licorice root
Grown in parts of Europe and Asia, licorice root is one of the most widely used herbs in Chinese medicine. It is very sweet as it contains a natural sweetener that is fifty times sweeter than sucrose. Licorice root helps the body adapt to stress and is great if you suffer from adrenal fatigue, as it has been found to help the body regulate cortisol (the stress hormone), which gives the adrenals a break. It can also be used to treat coughs, colds, and sore throats; help with circulation, digestive issues, and menopausal symptoms; and support liver, lung, and respiratory function.

Turmeric
Known as the wonder spice, it is also sometimes called Indian saffron or the golden spice. Probably the best-known adaptogen, most of us are likely to have a jar of ground turmeric on our kitchen shelves already. You can also get it as a fresh root, which you can juice or use in cooking. It is very high in antioxidants and its main active ingredient is curcumin. In Ayurvedic medicine, turmeric is used to ease chronic pain; reduce inflammation; improve liver function, digestion, and gut health; and as a preventative measure for cold, flu, and even cancer. Combining with black pepper or cayenne enhances the effects.

Holy basil
Actually a member of the mint family, despite its name, this queen of herbs has been used in Ayurvedic medicine for thousands of years to fight infections due to its antibacterial properties. It has also been shown in modern-day studies to help support a strong immune system. It's a great choice if you are feeling under the weather or are experiencing a period of stress or anxiety, and is a good source of vitamins A and C, calcium, zinc, and iron.

Breakfast banoffee pie jars

Is this breakfast or is it dessert—and does it really matter?! Although it looks and tastes super decadent, it is packed with health-promoting ingredients. Goji granola, bananas, peanut butter, dates, and a little grated chocolate—you're guaranteed to have a great start to the day.

Caramel:
2 tsp maple syrup
⅔ cup milk (I use almond)
1 tbsp peanut or almond butter
a handful of pitted dates (about 6), soaked in hot water for a few minutes and drained
a pinch of salt

7 tbsp oat-based whipping cream
7 tbsp vegan vanilla yogurt
1 tsp vanilla extract
2 large bananas, sliced
¼ cup Goji granola (page 15)
1 square of dark chocolate, grated (optional)

To make the caramel, put all the caramel ingredients in a blender and blend until smooth.

Using a handheld mixer, whisk the whipping cream until thick. Add the yogurt and vanilla extract.

In glass jars, make layers using the sliced banana, whipped yogurt, granola, and caramel. Top with a little grated dark chocolate if you like and enjoy.

Sweet potato pasta bake

Creamy and delicious, sweet potato makes the most incredible, velvety sauce that's perfect for coating pasta in this satisfying bake. Using mostly pantry ingredients, this is a great dish to pull together when you need something hearty and filling and to give you a lift after a long day.

14 ounces dried pasta
3 tbsp olive oil
1 red bell pepper, chopped
1 onion, chopped
1 tsp mixed dried herbs
1 tsp smoked paprika
1 slice of bread, crushed into crumbs

Sauce:
1 large sweet potato, washed, peeled, and chopped
13½-ounce can coconut milk
2 tbsp nutritional yeast
2 garlic cloves
a bunch of parsley, chopped
salt and pepper

Preheat the oven to 350°F on the convection setting.

Cook the pasta according to the package instructions, drain, and set aside.

Meanwhile, boil the sweet potato for about 10 minutes until soft, then drain and set aside.

Add the olive oil to a skillet over medium heat, add the bell pepper and onion, and cook for 5 minutes until soft. Mix with the drained pasta, herbs, and smoked paprika and set aside.

Blend the cooked sweet potato and the rest of the sauce ingredients in a blender until smooth and creamy. Add a little water if it seems too thick.

Add the sauce to the pasta, mix well, and pour into a baking dish. Top with the breadcrumbs and bake for 15 minutes, until the top is golden.

Gem's eggplant parmigiana

Whenever I cook my eggplant parmigiana, I get so much lovely feedback, so I couldn't wait to share it with you. Layers of sweet eggplant, creamy béchamel, and rich tomato sauce will make this an instant favorite in your home, too. My top tip is to be generous with the final layer of béchamel, as this will make it extra delicious. The tomato sauce is fantastic in so many other dishes too—like lasagna or as a pizza topping, or simply stirred into pasta. I often make the sauce ahead and keep some in the freezer.

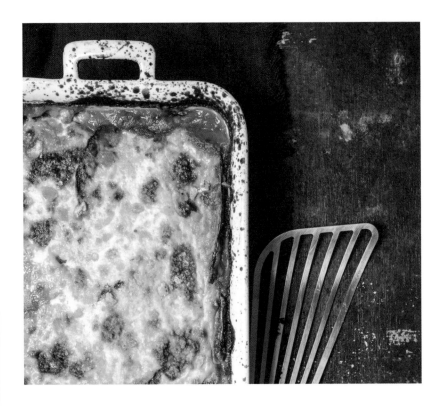

4 eggplants, cut lengthwise into ¼-inch-thick slices
2 tbsp olive oil
salt
⅓ cup breadcrumbs

Tomato sauce:
2 tbsp olive oil
1 onion, finely diced
4 large garlic cloves, finely diced
2x 14-ounce cans chopped tomatoes
7-ounce jar oil-packed sun-dried tomatoes, drained (but keep the oil for later) and chopped
1 fresh bay leaf
a handful of fresh basil leaves, chopped
1 tsp Italian seasoning
1 tsp sugar
salt and pepper

Béchamel:
3 tbsp vegan butter
2 tbsp all-purpose flour
2 cups plant-based milk
2 tbsp nutritional yeast
salt and pepper

Green salad, to serve

Preheat the oven to 400°F on the convection setting.

Place the eggplant slices on an unlined baking sheet, toss with a little olive oil and salt, and bake for 20 to 25 minutes, flipping them gently once halfway through the cooking time.

Meanwhile, make the tomato sauce by heating the olive oil in a large skillet over medium-high heat. Add the onion and garlic and cook until soft, 4 to 5 minutes. Add the tomatoes, sun-dried tomatoes, bay leaf, basil, herbs, and 1 cup water. Reduce the heat to medium-low and simmer for 20 minutes, until the sauce thickens and then add the sugar and season with salt and pepper.

To make the béchamel, melt the butter in a pan over medium heat, add the flour, and whisk until thickened; make sure it doesn't brown. Pour the milk into the pan and continue to whisk until the sauce is thickened. Add the nutritional yeast, season with salt and pepper, and stir.

To layer the parmigiana, start by spreading 1 cup of the tomato sauce over the bottom of a large baking dish. Follow with a layer of the eggplant slices and then 1½ cups of the tomato sauce and eggplant. Continue until you've used up all the sauce and eggplant.

Finish the last layer with the cheesy béchamel and scatter the breadcrumbs over the top.

Bake for 25 minutes until the top is nicely browned. Let stand for at least 30 minutes before you cut into slices and serve with a green salad.

Future-proofing your immunity

It's inevitable that we will hit times of ill-health—whether physical or mental—at some stage, even if it's just a cold or sore throat in the winter months, but doing all the groundwork beforehand means we can hopefully get back on our feet faster. The main ideas I've focused on in this book, and which I try to make sure I'm always on top of, are:

- **Eating a varied and healthy diet that includes lots of different whole grains, fruits, and veg.** This will ensure you're getting all the vitamins and minerals you need, as well as supporting good gut health—see page 100 for why supporting your gut is vital to good immunity.

- **Staying properly hydrated**—see pages 20–21 for more on this, as well as ideas for how to keep up your fluid intake.

- **Getting enough quality sleep.** I've learned the hard way how important it is to listen to my body and mind and to rest or take some extra time out to relax when I need it.

- **Factoring in regular exercise**—even if it's a gentle walk on the beach or a mess around with my kids in the park. Exercising outside is even better for you, as you get fresh air and a dose of vitamin D.

- **Reducing stressors in my life**—be that toxic people (see page 99), situations and habits that don't bring out the best in me, or overloading my days so I feel I'm no longer in control (see page 26). We all experience some stress in our lives, but trying to reduce it where possible can really impact your long-term health. A positive attitude really helps too—but not when it crosses over into toxic positivity: see page 186 for more on this and the dangers of comparison.

- **Community**—having a strong sense of community is now thought to be a major contributor to longevity and illness prevention. My network of friends and family are so important to me, as is making time to give back to others.

- **Washing my hands**—so simple I almost didn't include it here but washing our hands properly after we've been out and about is a really easy way to prevent ourselves picking up germs! See page 119 for my natural handwash recipe.

- **Turbocharging my immunity throughout the year with supplements and superfoods**, which I change through the seasons—e.g., including more vitamin D during the darker winter months. See pages 12–13, 109, and 164 for some of the ways I supercharge my diet.

Most importantly, I try to think about my immunity and overall well-being in a holistic, big-picture way, remembering it's all about balance—following the ancient Chinese philosophy of yin and yang. I make time to properly tune in to what my mind and body are telling me. So often we race through life and don't realize what we need until it's too late. I prioritize keeping my mind healthy just as much as my body, through yoga, breathwork, meditation, and self-reflection. And through this I often realize I need to change up my diet or that I need a bit more rest. Sometimes I realize I might need to take some more radical steps and make some bigger changes (see page 146).

Every day I reflect on everything I am grateful for—it is such a simple and powerful way to boost your mood and help you feel more optimistic about the future, which have both been proven to strengthen the immune system.

Super-boost rainbow curry + Brazil nuts + sweet ginger chutney

1 tbsp coconut oil
2 potatoes, cubed
14-ounce can chopped
    tomatoes
1 cup water
2 carrots, sliced
2 medium potatoes,
    peeled and cut into
    small cubes
1 red onion, chopped
⅓ cup frozen peas
1 green bell pepper,
    chopped into squares
1 red bell pepper,
    chopped into squares
3½ ounces green
    beans, trimmed and
    halved
1 cup Brazil nuts,
    chopped
3½ ounces baby
    spinach leaves

My mom always puts Brazil nuts in her curries and they add a whole new dimension to curry night! They are very high in selenium, which can improve your mood, and support the thyroid, which helps regulate the body's metabolism. They also add a lovely crunch and extra protein, while all the goodness from the rainbow veggies will supercharge your immune system and build strength. The apple and ginger chutney is so delicious, you can eat this with anything—I'm sure a spoonful is almost medicinal!

Curry paste:
1 green chile, chopped
2 garlic cloves
1-inch piece fresh
  ginger, peeled
½ tsp ground turmeric
1 small red chile,
  seeded
½ tsp garam masala
1 tsp ground coriander
2 tbsp olive oil
½ tsp ground cumin
a splash of water

Apple and ginger chutney:
2 tbsp olive oil
1-inch piece fresh
  ginger, peeled and
  finely chopped
4 cloves
3 apples, peeled,
  cored, and chopped
5 tbsp brown sugar
1 tsp red chile powder
7 tbsp apple cider
  vinegar
1 cup water

Make the curry paste: Combine all the ingredients in a blender and blend on high until a paste forms.

Melt the coconut oil in a large pan over medium heat. Add the curry paste and cook for a few minutes, stirring all the time. Add the potato and cook, stirring, for about 3 minutes. Add the chopped tomatoes and water and cook for another minute. Add the rest of the veggies (apart from the spinach), stir, and put a lid on. Turn down the heat to low and cook for about 20 minutes until the veggies are soft.

Meanwhile, make the chutney. Heat the oil in a large pan over medium-low heat. Add the ginger and the cloves and cook for 1 minute. Add the apple and cook for another 2 minutes over low heat.

Add the sugar, chile powder, and vinegar and stir. Add the water and cover the pan with a lid. Cook over low heat for 5 minutes, stirring occasionally.

The curry should be nearly ready, so add the Brazil nuts and spinach and cook for another few minutes.

Serve the curry in deep bowls topped with a spoonful of chutney.

High-vibe cleansing bowl + fermented pickles

When you want to feel part of the high-vibes club, the vibrant colors from all the gorgeous veg in this rice bowl will make you feel alive and boost your mood. Fermented pickles will give your gut some TLC (see pages 102–3) and the tahini dressing with garlic, ginger, honey, and turmeric will help protect your immunity. Prepare this on a Sunday and take it to work as a packed lunch for the next few days to keep those good vibes flowing.

1 butternut squash, peeled and cut into wedges
2 tbsp olive oil
a pinch of salt
1¾ cups brown rice
2 avocados, cubed
2 carrots, grated
4 cooked beets, cubed
3 handfuls of spinach
Gut-loving sauerkraut (page 103)
Carrot + ginger kimchi (page 103)

Dressing:
1 tbsp tahini
1 tbsp olive oil
1 garlic clove, finely chopped
½-inch piece fresh ginger, peeled and finely chopped
1 tbsp honey
1 tsp ground turmeric
juice of 1 lemon

Preheat the oven to 350°F on the convection setting. Line a baking sheet with parchment paper.

Toss the butternut squash wedges with the olive oil and a pinch of salt and arrange on the lined baking sheet. Roast for about 30 minutes, until golden and cooked through.

Meanwhile, make the dressing by adding all the dressing ingredients to a small bowl and whisking until combined.

Divide the cooked brown rice, avocado, carrot, beet, and spinach among four bowls. Add a spoonful of sauerkraut and/or kimchi and then generously drizzle with the dressing.

Cherry Bakewell slice + nice cream

Oh my goodness, this is the most delicious dessert and you are going to love it! It's best served warm with the nice cream, but if you have leftovers, then enjoy a slice the next day with a cup of tea. If you haven't got any frozen bananas, just pop them in the freezer for an hour.

⅔ cup vegan butter
⅔ cup sugar
1½ cups almond meal
1 cup plus
  2 tablespoons
  all-purpose flour
1½ tsp baking powder
1 tsp vanilla extract
1 tsp almond extract
¼ cup milk (I used
  almond)
7 ounces frozen
  cherries, defrosted
  and drained
¼ cup sliced almonds

Flax egg:
2 tbsp ground flaxseed
5 tbsp water

Nice cream:
3 bananas, frozen
2 tbsp milk of choice
1 tsp vanilla extract

Preheat the oven to 325°F on the convection setting. Line a 9-inch round cake pan with parchment paper cut to fit and grease the sides with coconut oil or butter.

Make a flax egg by mixing the ground flaxseed in a bowl with the water. Set aside until the mixture sets, about 10 minutes.

In a bowl, beat the butter and sugar together until light and fluffy. Add the rest of ingredients (except the cherries and almonds). Mix well.

Put half the mixture into the prepared cake pan, then top with the cherries. Pour in the other half of the batter and top with the almonds.

Bake for 45 minutes until the top is golden brown. Take the cake out of the oven and let cool for 10 minutes before removing it from the pan.

To make the nice cream, combine all the ingredients in a blender and blend for a few minutes until smooth. Serve immediately, or it in the freezer until needed.

SEAWEED AND SEA MOSS

Seaweed is one of my favorite superfoods. It has an amazing umami, salty flavor and is incredibly nutrient dense. It's a source of some hard-to-find vitamins and minerals, such as vitamins K and B12 and iodine, as well as high levels of potassium, magnesium, zinc, and iron. Seaweed supports thyroid function, which is vital for maintaining energy levels and repairing cells in your body, as well as being rich in antioxidants, which can help protect your cells from damage, fiber for good digestion, and omega-3s, which support good brain and heart health, and can reduce inflammation and even boost your mood.

I also love that there are so many ways you can eat it. I add it to stir-fries, soups, noodle dishes, and stews. It creates an amazing salted caramel taste in date and vanilla smoothies, you can blend it into hummus, or use nori sheets as wraps or sushi rolls to supercharge each one with nutrients and goodness. It's also a great seasoning alternative. I love making seaweed bread too—just add some dried flakes to your regular bread dough.

I buy my seaweed dried in packages, but you can buy it fresh or even forage for your own. Consult a local foraging expert before gathering your own so you know what you're doing. The main types of seaweed that are commonly available are dulse, kelp, mixed seaweed flakes, and nori sheets. You can use any of them in the recipes opposite.

Sea moss is a type of seaweed that grows around the Atlantic Ocean. Like other seaweeds, it is rich in nutrients and minerals—it contains 92 of the 102 minerals our body needs! It can help reduce inflammation and rid the body of mucus, so is great if you have a cold. It supports good gut health, and if you apply it to the skin, it can soothe eczema, psoriasis, and acne breakouts. It can also help balance hormone levels so is great for PMS and easing menopausal symptoms. I buy sea moss as a gel (you can also buy it in powdered form or capsules), which I add to hot water to make a tea or stir into broths and smoothies.

Since seaweed is so high in certain minerals, it's advised you eat it no more than three times per week. Iodine is essential for thyroid health, but too much can actually harm your thyroid; and vitamin K (which is good for blood clotting) can affect how certain blood-thinning medications work. Always check with your doctor if you're not sure.

Seaweed, kimchi + sriracha popcorn
—

SERVES 4 | *Prep time: 5 minutes*
Cook time: 5 minutes

2 tbsp finely chopped kimchi
1 tsp toasted sesame oil
1 tsp sriracha
a large bag of salted popcorn
1 sheet of nori roasted seaweed,
    or 2 tbsp dulse or kelp flakes

Mix the kimchi, oil, and sriracha in a bowl. Add the popcorn and mix well. Spread in a single layer on a parchment-lined baking sheet. Preheat the oven to 350°F (convection setting) and bake the popcorn for 5 minutes. Sprinkle with the seaweed and mix.

Super seaweed salad dressing
—

SERVES 4 | *Prep time: 5 minutes*

1 tbsp toasted sesame oil
1 tbsp soy sauce
1 tsp seaweed flakes
1 tbsp rice vinegar
1 tbsp brown sugar
a pinch of salt
1-inch piece fresh ginger, peeled and
    grated

Combine all the ingredients in a bowl and whisk well until creamy. Keep in a glass jar with a lid in a cool place for up to 2 weeks.

Toasted seaweed chips
—

SERVES 4 | *Prep time: 5 minutes*
Cook time: 8 minutes

10 sheets roasted nori seaweed
¼ cup soy sauce
4 tsp toasted sesame oil
a large pinch of red pepper flakes
    (optional)
cracked black pepper (optional

Preheat the oven to 300°F (convection setting). Line 2 or 3 baking sheets with parchment paper. Lay the nori shiny-side up on the parchment. Mix the soy sauce and oil in a bowl and brush onto each sheet of nori. Bake for 8 minutes. Let cool, then cut the sheets into 4 or 6 pieces. Add chile flakes or black pepper, if you like. Eat right away.

Seaweed butter
—

MAKES 1¼ CUPS | *Prep time: 5 minutes*

3 sheets roasted nori or 2 tbsp
    seaweed flakes (dulse, kelp, or
    a mix)
1¼ cups vegan butter, cubed

In a blender, finely grind the seaweed. Add the butter and blend until it is nicely whipped, then scrape onto a sheet of plastic wrap and roll it into a log. Twist both ends to tighten and secure with rubber bands. Refrigerate until firm. Store wrapped in plastic wrap in the fridge for 4 weeks.

CHAPTER 5

My Wellness Toolkit

Five tonics to keep you in balance 172

Elderberry winter tonic •
Ginger, lemon + garlic
honey • General strength-
ening health tonic •
Stomach-soothing tonic •
Parsley + ginger super
green tonic

Nutrition clusters 175

Sweet + salty nut clusters •
Peanut butter + puffed rice
bites • Stuffed-date super
snack

Brown-butter pasta +
crispy sage leaves 179

Golden sweet potato,
turmeric + almond creamy
soup 180

Sunshine fermented chia
pudding 183

Coconut blondies 184

My wellness toolkit

Think of this chapter as my collection of quick fixes that you can turn to when you need a helping hand or a comforting, reassuring hug. The recipes and ideas will benefit you at any stage of your wellness and immunity journey, but they're specifically designed for those days when you're just feeling a bit out of sorts. Maybe a work project has been stressing you out and you got home late, or you feel your energy levels have taken a bit of a dip lately, or perhaps you're in a bad mood for no particular reason. These are the ways I lift myself out of a dark mood, so I can feel like myself again as quickly as possible.

I say it all the time, but I think it's worth reminding ourselves of it again here too: make time to really listen to what your body and mind are telling you. Even if you are so busy—in fact, especially if you feel like you don't have a second to stop—sit down for five minutes somewhere quiet, close your eyes, and tune into yourself. It's almost like a super-mini power nap. You'll feel instantly more balanced and you'll be able to identify more easily what it is you need in order to feel more in control.

Pay attention to your emotions and respect your gut feeling—it's a real thing! If I can feel myself getting angry or upset, I always try to figure out why, so that I can resolve any issues and move on. Revisit some of the earlier sections in the book for ways to lean into what you're feeling (see page 146), or seek advice from someone you trust, a mentor, or a health professional. If we have a niggling feeling something isn't right, that's our body's way of telling us we need to make some changes. Get back to the essentials of good nutrition and other ways to boost your immunity (see page 156), and you'll be back on track in no time.

Plant powders

I often use plant powders in smoothies, juices, energy balls, or salad dressings, or in more general cooking, either to add an extra layer of nutrition or because I'm experiencing a specific health complaint at the time. The benefits of plant powders are wide-ranging—from increased energy to glowing skin—but they all support good immunity and provide intense boosts of vitamins and minerals. Powders are also usually a lot cheaper than branded supplements, but still provide all the benefits. Always buy from a trusted online health store and organic is best. Check the package for the recommended dosage, as potency can vary. I often split a daily dose between a smoothie in the morning (page 63) and a tea or juice later on.

My top seven plant powders

Baobab powder
Very nutrient-dense, baobab powder is rich in vitamins B and C and iron, as well as calcium, potassium, and magnesium. Baobab seeds also contain omega-3s, -6s, and -9s, which are great for fighting inflammation and for easing skin conditions (see page 59 for more on healthy fats).

Cacao powder and cacao nibs
High in antioxidants and an amazing source of potassium, magnesium, and iron, they are a great mood booster while providing immunity support—as well as tasting delicious!

Goji berry powder
Goji berries have been used in traditional medicine for centuries to ward off illness and infection and naturally enhance the immune system. They are also very high in protein for a fruit. I often eat these whole too, as a snack or in the Goji granola on page 15.

Maca powder
Maca is an amazing superfood, especially for women, as it can help balance hormone levels, easing PMS, or menopausal symptoms. It can also increase your libido, lift your mood, boost your energy levels, enhance your immune system, and improve memory.

Moringa powder
The moringa tree has so many life-giving powers that it is known in some cultures as the "tree of life." It is anti-inflammatory and contains an incredible amount of vitamins—seven times more vitamin C than oranges, super-high levels of calcium, potassium, magnesium, and iron, as well as vitamins A, B, D, and E and several minerals. It's also packed with antioxidants. It is believed to have antibiotic and antibacterial properties too, so can protect against infection, as well as easing inflammation and joint pain, helping with allergy or asthma symptoms, and supporting your digestion. It can also balance hormones and is amazing for your skin! An all-around superhero of a superfood!

Nettle powder
Nettle powder is probably the plant powder I take most often, and I swear by its abilities. High in amino acids, protein, flavonoids, and bone-building minerals like iron, calcium, magnesium, potassium, and zinc, it helps support your overall health and immunity, your sleep, and your skin. It's relatively inexpensive too, so it is a great everyday superfood. Perfect if you're feeling a bit run-down as it can give you such a boost—add to homemade nut milk (page 14) or any of the smoothies on page 63.

Pine pollen
Known to have antiaging properties and for helping to reduce fatigue, it also boosts the hormone testosterone, so can help support you if you are going through menopause, when testosterone levels decline.

FIVE TONICS TO KEEP YOU IN BALANCE

Strengthening and restorative, herbal tonics have been used for thousands of years across many cultures around the world. Some tonics are designed to help with specific concerns, while others provide key ingredients that aim to keep your entire system functioning at its best. The idea is that you drink tonics before an issue occurs, in order to help reduce any potential symptoms and support your immunity. So if you know you're about to head into a busy patch, the people around you are sniffling, or you just feel you could do with a helping hand, these could be just the tonic you need.

Elderberry winter tonic

—

Helps support your immunity and combat cold/flu symptoms.

—

A simple immunity-boosting and delicious elderberry syrup with dried elderberries, honey, and spices. Can be used medicinally or drizzled over pancakes or waffles as a sweet treat. Have 1 tablespoon a day. I give this to my kids daily from September through March and they love it.

MAKES 2 CUPS | *Prep time: 15 minutes*
Cook time: 1 hour

4 cups water
3½ ounces dried elderberry
2-inch piece fresh ginger, peeled
  and grated
1 tsp ground cinnamon
½ tsp ground cloves
1 cup raw honey

Add the water, elderberries, ginger, cinnamon, and cloves to a pan. Bring to a boil over high heat, cover, reduce the heat to low, and simmer for 1 hour until the liquid has reduced by half. Remove from the heat and cool, then mash the berries using a spoon. Strain the mixture into a glass jar and let the liquid cool. Add the honey and stir well, then store the syrup in the fridge for up to 6 weeks.

Ginger, lemon + garlic honey

—

Helps with viral, bacterial, and yeast infections.

—

Take 1 or 2 teaspoons per day to help prevent colds and flu, or if you are actively fighting an infection take 1 teaspoon every 3 to 4 hours until you feel better.

MAKES ⅔ CUP | *Prep time: 5 minutes*

10 garlic cloves, peeled
3-inch piece fresh ginger, peeled
  (or 2 tbsp ground ginger)
3 unwaxed lemons, cut in half
2 tbsp honey (manuka is great if you
  can get it)

Blend all the ingredients until you have a smooth paste. Pour into a clean jar and store in the fridge for up to 2 weeks.

General strengthening health tonic

—

A great all-around tonic to energize, fortify, and keep your immunity up.

—

Keep in the fridge for up to 2 months and have a shot daily.

MAKES 1½ CUPS | *Prep time: 10 minutes*

6 garlic cloves, chopped
2 onions, chopped
2-inch piece fresh ginger, grated
2-inch piece fresh horseradish root, grated
1 tsp cayenne pepper
1½ cups raw apple cider vinegar
1 tbsp honey

Put all the ingredients in a jar with a lid and shake well to mix. Store in a cool, dark place for 2 weeks, shaking the jar at least once a day. Strain the tonic through cheesecloth or a fine-mech sieve before storing in the fridge.

Stomach-soothing tonic

—

This will really help with nausea and sickness, and also aids good digestion. Great for morning sickness and hangovers.

—

Keep in the fridge for up to a week, to sip on regularly as needed.

MAKES 2 CUPS | *Prep time: 10 minutes*

1 fennel tea bag
15 mint leaves
2-inch piece fresh ginger, peeled and grated
juice of 1 lemon

Boil 2 cups water and pour over the fennel tea and mint leaves in a large teapot. Let cool. Once cooled, strain into a jar and mix in the ginger and lemon juice. Keep in the fridge and drink chilled, to settle your tummy.

Parsley + ginger super green tonic

—

Helps reduce any inflammation in the body.

—

Parsley can help reduce bloating and is high in antioxidants, so acts as an anti-inflammatory. Make this one fresh and drink it immediately.

MAKES 2 CUPS | *Prep time: 5 minutes*

a bunch of fresh parsley
2-inch piece fresh ginger, peeled
1¼ cups water
juice of 1 lemon

Add the parsley, ginger, and water to a blender, then blend until smooth. Add the fresh lemon juice.

Nutrition clusters

Small but mighty, these four pocket-sized snacks are packed with energy and nutrition. Perfect to carry with you for emergency fuel.

Sweet + salty nut clusters
—
Almonds (and hazelnuts) are very rich in vitamin E, which helps boost the immune system.

MAKES 15 | *Prep time: 5 minutes*
Cook time: 20 minutes

2 cups unsalted mixed nuts (walnuts,
    pecans, almonds)
2½ cups ground almonds
a large pinch of salt
3 tbsp maple syrup

Topping:
salt

· Preheat the oven to 340°F (convection setting) and line a baking sheet with parchment paper.

· In a bowl, add all the ingredients and mix well, until all the nuts are coated. Using a spoon, scoop clusters of the mixture onto a baking sheet with space between each one. Bake for 20 minutes.

· When you take them out of the oven, sprinkle with salt and let cool. They will become crisp once cooled. Keep in an airtight container for up to 4 weeks.

Variation: Coconut + super seed munchies
—
Seeds, in particular sunflower seeds, are high in zinc and selenium, a lack of which can leave us experiencing low moods.

Follow the recipe above, swapping the mixed nuts for 1⅓ cups mixed seeds and 1¼ cups coconut flakes.

Image on page 177 →

Peanut butter + puffed rice bites

—

Full of protein and good fats from the nut butter and energy from the oats and maple syrup. These are fun to make too, so if you have kids, get them involved.

MAKES 15 | *Prep time: 15 minutes*
Chill time: 20 minutes

¼ cup peanut butter
¼ cup honey or maple syrup
½ tsp vanilla extract
a pinch of salt
3⅓ cups puffed rice
½ cup oats

· Melt the peanut butter and honey in a pan over medium heat and stir until creamy. Add the mixture to a large bowl and stir in the puffed rice and oats.

· Using a tablespoon, scoop out a spoonful and roll it into a ball.

· Place the balls on a plate and put in the fridge for about 20 minutes to firm.

· These will keep in an airtight container in the fridge for up to 2 weeks.

Stuffed-date super snack

—

Dates are my wonder fruit. They not only taste amazing but are rich in protective antioxidants and high in fiber as well. They are also high in vitamin K, so they're great for bone and blood health.

All these fillings are my favorites, but I would suggest you play around with flavors as dates go so well with lots of foods and are a great sugar replacement in cooking too.

MAKES 20 | *Prep time: 5 minutes*

20 large dates, pitted

Filling options:
Peanut butter + a sprinkle of ground cinnamon
Cream cheese mixed with chopped sun-dried tomato and fresh basil
Sweet + salty nut clusters (page 175), cut in half

· Cut the dates lengthwise. Use a spoon to fill each date evenly with your chosen filling mixture.

· Eat some right away and store the rest in an airtight container in the fridge for up to 2 weeks.

*Peanut butter +
puffed rice bites*

*Sweet + salty
nut clusters*

*Coconut + super seed
munchies*

Brown-butter pasta + crispy sage leaves

This is my SOS emergency pasta. On the table in fifteen minutes and using ingredients I always have in my cupboards and fridge, it is heaven on a plate and gives everyone a real energy boost while being gentle to digest. It's my absolute go-to when I don't know what I feel like eating and a large bowl provides an instant pick-me-up. Crispy sage tastes amazing and makes a simple bowl of pasta feel extra special, but you can use a teaspoon of dried sage instead—or leave it out altogether.

10½ ounces dried
   pasta (e.g.,
   tagliatelle)
¾ cup vegan butter
8 fresh sage leaves
   or 1 tsp dried sage
   (optional)
1 garlic clove, minced
¼ tsp salt
1 tbsp fresh lemon juice
⅔ cup veggie stock
Vegan parmesan
   (page 19; optional)
salt and freshly ground
   mixed peppercorns

Fill a large pan with water, put the lid on, and bring to a boil over high heat. Add the pasta and cook for 8 to 10 minutes.

Meanwhile, melt the butter in a pan over medium heat and cook until the butter starts to brown. Add the sage leaves and fry for a few seconds. Remove from the heat and add the garlic. Cook for a few minutes to crisp up the sage leaves and brown the garlic, but make sure they don't burn. Add the salt, lemon juice, and veggie stock and cook for a few more minutes.

Drain the pasta and mix it into the sauce. Season to taste with salt and pepper and serve in large pasta bowls, topped with my Vegan parmesan if you like.

Golden sweet potato, turmeric + almond creamy soup

Luxurious, rich, and oh so tasty! The almonds give this soup a lovely creaminess and the spices will keep your immune system strong. Sweet potatoes are rich in fiber to help your digestive system and the garlic, ginger and turmeric are full of health-giving properties. A bowl of this golden soup will leave you glowing from within.

---

4 medium sweet potatoes, scrubbed and chopped into quarters

4 tsp coconut oil, melted

½ tsp salt, plus more to taste

¾ cup crushed almonds

1 medium white onion, chopped

2 garlic cloves, chopped

1-inch piece fresh ginger, peeled and chopped

1-inch piece fresh turmeric, peeled and chopped, or ½ tsp ground

4 cups veggie stock

salt and pepper

Preheat the oven to 400°F on the convection setting. Line a baking sheet with parchment paper.

Rub the sweet potatoes with 2 teaspoons of the coconut oil and season with salt. Place on the lined baking sheet and roast for 30 to 40 minutes until soft. Remove from the oven and set aside.

Spread the almonds over another baking sheet and toast in the oven on the bottom rack for about 5 minutes, making sure they don't burn. Let cool. Set a few aside for garnish.

Meanwhile, melt the remaining 2 teaspoons coconut oil in a medium pan over medium heat. Add the onion and cook for 5 minutes until softened. Then add the garlic, ginger, and turmeric and cook for 2 more minutes. Add the roasted sweet potato, almonds, and stock. Season with salt and pepper and stir well. Simmer over low heat for 10 minutes. Blend until smooth.

Pour into bowls and serve with some of the toasted almonds on top.

Sunshine fermented chia pudding

Such a pretty pudding that makes you feel like the sun is shining on you! Kefir is full of probiotics to support a healthy gut and boost your immune system, so this pudding is great to eat if you are taking or have recently taken antibiotics. You can also use other fruits, such as pineapple, berries, tropical fruit, oranges, and clementines—canned fruits are perfect for this, too.

2 ripe mangoes, diced
1 cup nondairy kefir (or you can use coconut milk)
¾ cup chia seeds

To serve:
1 tbsp coconut yogurt
1 tbsp Toasted nuts or seeds (page 19) or Goji granola (page 15)

In a blender, puree the mango until very smooth, 20 to 30 seconds. In a bowl, mix the pureed mango, kefir, and chia seeds. Stir to evenly distribute the chia seeds and prevent them from clumping together.

Pour the mixture into a jar with a lid and gently shake to prevent clumping. Place the jar in the fridge to chill for at least an hour and up to 3 days. I like to serve with a dollop of coconut yogurt and toasted nuts or seeds or goji granola on top.

Coconut blondies

My hero treat that I make when I want to impress because they taste divine but are super easy! A little goes a long way and they're guaranteed to satisfy any sweet-toothed munchie attack. Ideal for a quick power-up.

¾ cup all-purpose flour
1 tsp baking powder
scant ½ cup almond flour
⅓ cup unsweetened shredded coconut
2 tbsp chia seeds
⅓ cup packed brown sugar
1 cup milk of choice
3 tbsp peanut butter

Optional extras:
⅓ cup white chocolate chunks
½ cup dried cranberries
½ cup chopped walnuts

Preheat the oven to 350°F on the convection setting and line a 7-inch square baking sheet with parchment paper.

In a bowl, stir together all the dry ingredients. Then add the milk and peanut butter and your optional extra and mix until smooth. I use a handheld mixer.

Pour into the baking sheet and bake for 25 minutes until firm. Allow to cool in the pan for about 15 minutes and then place carefully on a cooling rack.

Slice into squares and store in an airtight container at room temperature for up to 5 days.

REMEMBER YOU'RE AMAZING JUST THE WAY YOU ARE!

I always try to have a positive attitude to life and count my blessings—and this has also been identified as one of the key ways to support a strong immune system. But telling yourself and the people around you that "everything will be OK" or to "look on the bright side" when things go wrong is not always helpful. The ethos of the "positive-vibes-only club" can actually feel incredibly dismissive of someone's experiences, including your own, and can prevent you from working through difficult emotions.

Setbacks will occur in life and things won't always work out as planned. Sometimes things just won't be OK—or at least not the way you expected—but it's part of life to find ways to overcome those challenges and to learn from them. We all have ups and downs when it comes to our mood, and sometimes all we need is a little time to reflect and recharge, to allow ourselves to sit with those difficult feelings in order to process them and come out the other side feeling happier, stronger, and more resilient. Those feelings are telling you something important, so listen to what's making you uncomfortable and create some action points to tackle them head on.

In turn, support those around you who may be going through tough times by listening and letting them know their feelings are valid. Experiencing low moods can significantly affect our overall sense of well-being, and anxiety and worry can often mean our sympathetic nervous system is active, which reduces our ability to heal and fight off infection (see page 46). So it's vital to keep on top of how we feel and address any low moods proactively.

Something else we all do every day that is not always good for us is to compare ourselves with others. We are constantly exposed to insights into other people's worlds, especially through social media—where everything looks like it's going great every single day—and it's often impossible not to find ourselves judging our own lives against what we see. Although we know that those are just highlights, it's hard not to compare where we are in life or what we're doing. But that's a surefire way to feel inadequate—there will always be someone doing something bigger or more impressive on any given day, but remember it's not real life.

Don't give in to it! Comparison can be an indication that you need approval from others, so try to stay focused on your own path and don't worry about what everyone else is doing—everyone's life is different and we all do things at our own pace. Revisit your core priorities (see pages 57 and 99) or create a new vision board (see page 137) to regain your focus if you feel you need to bring yourself back to who you are. Remember that literally no one is perfect and everyone has moments of insecurity. You never really know what is going on in someone else's life and we're all just doing the best we can—and you can't ask for more than that!

Index

adaptogens 148–9
almonds 10, 14, 15, 18, 19, 59, 63, 73, 104, 162, 175, 180
amino acids 148, 171
antiaging 110, 149, 171
antibacterial properties 13, 92, 138, 149, 171
antioxidants 60, 76, 100, 101, 109, 113, 139, 148, 149, 174, 176
anxiety 12, 13, 35, 46, 72, 148
apple cider vinegar 100
apples 33, 34, 159
ashwagandha 148
eggplants 154–5
avocados 18, 29, 59, 85, 86, 122, 161

bananas 28, 60, 101
    recipes 63, 73, 126, 150, 162
barley 60, 76, 112, 122
basil 12, 18, 20
beans 60, 101, 122
    black beans 85
    cannellini beans 49
    butter beans 49, 79, 107
beans and legumes 10, 59, 60, 61, 101
beets 34, 63, 67, 107, 161
berries 10, 17, 63, 129, 170
    breakfast 15, 73, 104, 141
beta-carotene 34
blueberries 139
Brazil nuts 14, 159
bread 17, 28, 164
breakfast recipes 53, 72, 104, 141, 150

breathing 35, 46–8
broccoli 50, 53, 60, 123

cabbage 87, 103
cacao 11, 14, 18, 129, 170
calcium 50, 61, 149, 170, 171
carrots 103
    juices 34
    meals 49, 67, 76, 79, 107, 122, 159, 161
    snacks and sides 87, 103
    soups 41, 74, 113
cashews 14, 19, 142
cauliflower 67, 86, 122
CBD oil 13, 38
celeriac 107
celery 33, 41, 49, 74, 79, 113, 126
chard 79, 123
cherries 17, 129, 162
chia seeds 17, 59, 62, 104, 129, 141, 183
chickpeas 15, 74, 79, 122
chiles 12, 126, 159
chocolate 11, 59, 129, 150
cholesterol 148, 149
cleaning 116, 117, 119
coconut 10, 15, 59, 175, 184
    water 21, 34, 63
cold-water therapy 147
colds 13, 28, 30, 33, 44, 45, 63, 138, 149, 164, 173
concentration 49, 110, 148, 149
coughs 44, 138, 149
cucumbers 21, 33, 103, 122

dates 63, 73, 104, 150, 176
digestion 20, 28, 41, 49, 53, 79, 100, 102, 138, 139
    see also gut health
dressings 19, 123, 161, 165, 170

echinacea 13
endorphins 147
energy
    boosting 18, 28, 42, 73, 110, 148, 174
    resetting 92
Epsom salts 13, 38
exercise 39, 71, 80–1, 99, 108

fatigue 50, 60, 171
fats, healthy 14, 18, 59, 122, 176
fermented foods 100, 102–3, 123, 161, 183
fiber 49, 62, 76, 101, 176, 180
flu 45, 63, 138, 173
frozen foods 12–13, 21, 62
fruits 10, 20, 21, 60, 62, 101, 156, 183

garlic 12, 79, 101
ginger 12, 28
    dressings 19, 165
    drinks 33, 34, 44, 45, 63, 138, 173, 174
    kimchi 103
    meals 42, 53, 64, 86, 112, 113, 114, 124, 126, 159, 161, 180
    sweet treats 30, 73, 91

ginseng 148
goji berries 15, 104, 170
grains 10, 60, 122
greens 50, 59, 60, 123
gut health 60, 100–1, 110, 142

hazelnuts 14, 18, 175
headaches 34, 49, 50
heart 59, 149
hemp 59, 67, 104
herbs 12, 92–3, 148, 149
holy basil 149
hydration 20–21, 44–5

immunity, boosting 12, 18,
   19, 34, 44, 46–8, 59, 104,
   113, 156–7
   adaptogens 148–9
   drinks 62–3, 138–9
   mushrooms 109, 110
   plant powders 170–1
inflammation, reducing
   33, 34, 59, 63, 110, 148,
   170, 174
iodine 59, 63, 164
iron 33, 50, 59, 63, 79, 112,
   149, 164, 171

joy, finding 134–7
juices 33–4, 138–9, 170

kale 42, 59, 79, 124–5
   drinks 33, 63
   soups 50, 113
   stir-fries 114, 142
kefir 101, 183
kimchi 100, 103, 142, 161, 165
kombucha 100

leeks 49, 50
lemons 15, 49, 76, 113, 141
   dressings 18, 161
   drinks 20, 21, 34, 44, 45,
      138, 173
   soups 50, 74
lentils 53, 60, 101, 113, 126
limes 30, 34, 45, 63, 85, 86,
   126, 139
liquid aminos 11
licorice root 149
living space 116–17

maca 14, 15, 171
magnesium 38, 50, 63, 72,
   76, 79, 164, 170, 171
mangoes 20, 30, 60, 63,
   86, 183
Marmite 29
massage 82, 83
meditation 35, 39, 137
melatonin 17, 72
menopause 71, 149,
   164, 171
minerals 13, 61, 62, 171
mint 12, 20, 34, 44, 45,
   86, 174
miso 11, 15, 19, 21, 28, 41,
   101, 112, 124–5
moringa powder 171
mushrooms 11, 29, 41, 61,
   76, 112, 114, 124–5, 142
   medicinal 13, 38, 62,
      109–11, 114

nausea 28, 34, 41, 45, 63, 73,
   138, 174
nettle powder 14, 171

noodles 10, 41, 114, 122,
   124–5
nourish bowls 121–3
nutritional yeast 11
nuts 10, 38, 59, 60, 61, 62,
   122, 142
   recipes 14, 18, 19, 104, 175
   see also individual nut
      entries

oatmeal 38, 72–3
oats 15, 38, 67, 72, 104, 176
oils 11–12
   essential 13, 21, 71, 83, 119
omega-3s 59, 164, 170
onions 101
oranges 30, 34, 63, 129, 138

parsley 174
pasta 10, 153, 179
peanut butter 15, 63, 150,
   176, 184
peas 41, 112, 159
peppers 60, 64, 87, 153, 159
period pains 50
pickles 100, 102–103, 161
pine pollen 171
pineapples 20, 60, 63, 68, 139
plant powders 170–1
plantain chips 123
plants 117, 118
PMS 44, 50, 71, 164, 171
potassium 60, 164, 170, 171
potatoes 41, 59, 74, 76,
   79, 159
prebiotics 60, 100, 101
probiotics 28, 41, 60, 63,
   100, 01, 102, 142, 183

protein 14, 15, 53, 60, 122, 159, 170, 171
puddings 68, 129, 141, 145, 150, 162, 183
pumpkin seeds 14, 17, 19, 59, 104, 122

quinoa 122

radishes 103
rice 41, 53, 114, 122, 161
rosemary 20, 93

saffron 44, 63
sage 92, 93, 179
sauerkraut 100, 103, 161
seaweed 11, 59, 100, 164–5
    drinks 21
    meals 114, 124–5
    snacks and sides 15, 142, 165
seeds 10, 19, 38, 59, 61
    see also individual seed entries
selenium 14, 60, 76, 110, 159, 175
self-care 24–7, 35–9, 46–8, 56–8, 70–1, 80–3, 96–100, 108, 116–17, 134–7, 156–7
serotonin 28, 82, 100, 129
sickness 45, 63, 174
skin 44, 71, 110, 118, 164, 170, 171
sleep, aiding 28, 38–9, 59, 71, 171

smoothies 62–3, 170, 171
soups 40–3, 50, 64, 74, 113, 180
soy sauce (tamari) 11
spices 12, 20, 53
spinach 41, 53, 76, 123, 159, 161
    soups 41, 50, 113
squashes 15, 64, 122, 124–5, 161
stock 10
stress 59, 82, 98, 109, 134, 148, 149
sunflower seeds 15, 17, 19, 59, 175
superfoods 12, 14, 15, 62, 109, 164
sweet potatoes 15, 49, 67, 85, 113, 122, 153, 180

teas 38, 44, 45, 170, 174
tempeh 101
temperature, body 39
throats, sore 34, 44, 138, 149
thyroid 59, 159, 164
toast 28–9, 79
tofu 41, 59, 60, 122, 124–5
tomatoes 21, 49, 60, 67, 79, 85, 113, 122, 155, 159
tonics 172–4
toxins, removing 48, 53
turmeric 30, 34, 149
tzatziki 122

umami paste 11
uplift 56, 70–1, 92, 171

vinegars 11, 100, 119
vitamins 33, 62, 148
    A 149, 171
    B 111, 112, 170, 171
    B12 29, 60, 63, 164

    C 21, 30, 34, 38, 60, 63, 64, 149, 170, 171
    D 61, 63, 80, 110, 171
    E 171, 175
    K 50, 164, 176
    supplements 13, 61

walnuts 19, 59, 67, 104, 175, 184
weak, feeling 29, 49, 60, 63
whole grains 59, 101, 156

zinc 61, 63, 112, 149, 164, 175
zucchini 50, 53, 123

About Gem

Gem grew up as the youngest child of five, and is used to being around a lot of noise and chaos. She learned to cook from her mum, who is not only a fantastic cook but also taught her how to stick to a budget. Gem would often cook for her whole family from the age of eight years, and this is where her passion for food started.

During her teenage years Gem suffered from anorexia, but luckily recovered with love and support from family and friends, and made the connection that eating good foods could help with the healing process. Most of her twenties she spent partying and not looking after herself, and in her early thirties she experienced several miscarriages. Through these experiences, Gem worked out the link between eating well and feeling better, both physically and mentally. She started eating more plant-based foods and discovered their power to improve her physical health and boost her mood.

Being blessed with two healthy children was a real turning point, and after working in the mental health sector as a drug counselor for years, Gem and her family decided to head to Barcelona for an adventure and ended up staying for 2½ years. Gem set up a vegan takeout business from their apartment, preparing bento boxes for international DJs.

Cooking and following a plant-based whole-food diet in the sunshine felt good, and she started playing around with ingredients and developing recipes. Word spread and the business took off. In 2016, Gem and her family moved back to Brighton, where Gem's Wholesome Kitchen was born. Gem is known for her Nourish package—a bespoke delivery service of plant-based foods to nourish the mind and body. During the Covid-19 pandemic, she set up Gem's Community Kitchen, which supports vulnerable members of the community through education and fundraising projects.

Since writing her first book, *The Self-Care Cookbook*, Gem has been learning more about the power of plants and how they can help the healing process and prevent illness by supercharging the immune system. Gem believes diet and nutrition play a massive part in overall health and mental health and hopes this book inspires you.

Gem loves nothing more than cooking up a feast to share with family and friends that tastes good, boosts the mood, and supercharges the immune system. Like her food, Gem is bright, colorful, and full of love.

Thank you

Thank you to Laura Bayliss, and to the wonderful team at Vermilion for giving me this opportunity, and for being such a dream to work with.

Thank you to my amazing daughter, Carmen, for her brilliant illustrations. She worked so hard on these and I am so proud to have them in my book.

Thank you to my family, Peter, Carmen, and Hendrix, for supporting me always. I couldn't have written this book without them and all the cups of tea they brought me.

Thanks to Xavi Buendia and Emma Croman for taking the photos, and Katie de Toney for styling. You were all so much fun to work with, and I love the photos.

Thanks to all my followers and customers who have supported me and my business, and everyone who has bought my books.

Thanks to my mum for teaching me to cook from such a young age and never minding me getting messy.